RUNLOG

Diary and Guide for the Runner

John Cronin
Tim Houts

Specially printed for

_____

by

SPORTSLOG
p u b l i s h e r s

Designed and printed in the United States.
Cover photograph and all other photographs © 1993 Victah Sailer, Agence Shot
Cover and book design by Heidi Sandison.

Please direct any questions, comments or suggestions to:
Sports Log Publishers, P.O. Box 9275, South Laguna, CA 92677
(714) 376-0651, (800) 327-6303.

ISBN 0-9624232-4-6

Cover Photo: Martin Pitayo (2) and Antonio Niemczak (3) battle it out in the 1990 Chicago Marathon. Pitayo won. Photo by Victah Sailer.

About the authors

John Cronin

John Cronin has run competitive track and field and cross country for over 10 years, including an NCAA career at San Diego State University where he ran 1:49 for the 800 meter and 3:49 1500 meter.

John currently coaches middle and long distance runners at Saddleback College in Southern California. You can still see John at local 10k's and 5k's, although he prefers shorter distances.

Tim Houts

Tim Houts has run numerous 10k's and marathons since he began running in 1979 after ending his water polo career at Stanford University. Despite growing up as a competitive swimmer, Tim has posted a 37:30 10k, 3:30 marathon and has placed in the top fifth of his age group in international distance triathlons.

Introduction and preface to the third edition

Introduction

Welcome to *Run Log*.

We created *Run Log* to have all the features we as competitive runners always wanted in a diary: plenty of space to write down all the details of a run; concise and helpful training information; and inspirational photos to keep us motivated throughout the year.

Note your running plateaus, valleys and peaks in the diary. Use the training information in the guide to bring you faster times and increased performance. And enjoy the photos featured throughout the book.

Preface to the Third Edition

First, thank you for making *Run Log* so successful! Thanks to your terrific support and great suggestions we've sold out of two printings and are now on our third edition in less than two years. Second, here's a summary of the improvements in this edition:

All new photos

This edition features 24 ALL NEW color and black & white photos from this year's events to offer inspiration and movtivation. Enjoy.

Expanded Race Results Summary

Thanks to your comments, we've expanded the Race Results Summary pages to give you even more room to note your race results.

Easier-to-use Map to Raceday Worksheet

We've re-designed the Map to Raceday Worksheet to make planning for your events even easier.

Thanks again for your support. Good luck on a great season of training and racing!

John Cronin and Tim Houts

Table of Contents

PART I: TRAINING GUIDE

Stretching 1
Nutrition 2
Endurance training 4
Running for strength 6
Speed work 9
Surviving injuries 12
Fun runs and overtraining 14
Other books to read 15
Getting more out of your diary 16
How to use charts 17
Training/Race pace chart 19
Interval pace chart 20
Map to raceday chart 21
Race results summary chart 24
Cumulative mileage graph 26

PART II: TRAINING DIARY

Daily training diary pages 28

Stretching

Stretching increases flexibility, improves your running performance and helps prevent injury. Stretch before and after each run.

Stretch for flexibility

There are many exercises to stretch your body, but the basics work the best:

Hurdler's Stretch

To stretch your hamstrings, sit on the floor with your right leg bent back, almost under your buttock. Place your left leg straight out in front. Slowly stretch your left leg by trying to touch your nose to your left knee. Never "bounce" to stretch. Hold the position for 30 seconds.

To stretch your quadriceps, from the same position, slowly lean your body back toward the point where your shoulders reach the floor. Hold for 30 seconds.

Switch right and left leg positions and repeat to stretch the right leg's hamstrings and the left leg's quadriceps.

Back and Hamstring Stretch

To stretch your hamstrings and your back, sit on the floor and place both legs straight in front, knees flat on the floor, toes pointed to the ceiling. Slowly bend at the waist and try to touch your nose to your knees. Hold for 30 seconds.

To stretch your back, while lying on your back, bring your right knee toward your chest and roll it over toward the floor next to your left arm. Hold for 15 seconds. Repeat with left knee.

Calf Stretch

To stretch your calf, stand facing a wall and place your palms against the wall, above your head.   Place your right foot flat on the floor, away from the wall, while supporting yourself primarily on your bent left leg. Keep your right leg straight. Gently move your hips forward. Reverse right and left leg positions and repeat to stretch left calf.

Incorporate other muscle specific stretches as necessary. Get into the habit of stretching. A flexible body is less prone to injury, runs smoother and recovers faster.

Nutrition

Good, sound nutrition is a critical element to any training program. You want your body lean and well-fueled to train and race your best.

Remember these nutritional basics to keep your training on track:

Eat a balanced diet
A balanced diet includes: (1) carbohydrates, (2) proteins, (3) fats, and (4) vitamins and minerals.

Carbohydrates
Complex carbohydrates provide an excellent source of highly burnable "fuel" for training and racing, and often are a good source of protein, minerals and vitamins as well. Make carbohydrates 50-60% of your caloric intake.

Carbohydrates include: potatoes, rice, pasta, kasha, corn, peas, beans, and fruits and vegetables.

Proteins
Proteins provide a source to build and maintain strong bones and muscles. Make proteins 15% of your caloric intake.

Recent studies suggest that athletes in peak training may need up to 2 1/2 times the normal intake of protein to offset muscle breakdown. Adjust your protein intake to what works best for you.

Proteins include: meats, poultry, fish, cheese, beans and legumes (which are also carbohydrates), and whole wheat grains.

Fats
Fats, in limited quantity, are important to your body make-up. However, fats (like cheese and salad oil) contain more than twice the calories, ounce for ounce, than protein or carbohydrates. Limit your caloric fat intake to 25-30% of your total calories.

Fats include: butter, cheese, vegetable oils, fried foods, peanut butter, and olives.

Vitamins and minerals
Get all the vitamins and minerals you need in a well-balanced diet with plenty of fresh vegetables and fruits. Although all the vitamins and minerals needed by the human body can be found in a well balanced diet, consider vitamin supplements to offset deficiencies. Adjust your diet and supplements to what works best for you.

Limit sugars

Sugars like those in soft drinks and candy are empty calories which don't provide any nutritious value.

Limit sugars such as: chocolate, alcohol, hard candy, cake, cookies, pie, frozen yogurt, non-diet soft drinks, pancake syrup, jams, jellies, brown sugar, raw sugar, and foods containing sucrose or fructose.

Water is critical

When considering fluid replacement options, remember that the most important element to replace during any run is water. Water is critical to the body's cooling system. You'll become dehydrated if you don't replenish your body's water. Dehydration symptoms include: cramping, nausea, light headedness, and fatigue to the point of collapse in extreme cases. None of these improve your finish place or time.

As a general rule, drink 4-6 ounces water every 15 minutes during a long run or race. Adjust your water intake to the weather conditions and what works best for you.

Sports drinks/bars help for long efforts

Your body will burn through your available blood sugar, or carbohydrates, in events longer than 1 1/2 - 2 hours. Take a sports drink or energy bar as needed for events longer than 1 1/2 hours.

Limit the sports drink to no more than 5-10% sugar/carbohydrate (90-95% water) to maximize fluid absorption and prevent dehydration. Find the sports drink/bar that works best for you. Take the sports drink or bar on several training runs before you ever consider using it in a race. A race is the last place you want to find out how your body reacts to a particular sports drink or bar.

Evaluate your diet

Track your diet for one week every six to nine months to see if your diet is made up of 55–60% carbohydrates, 15% proteins, and 25–30% fats. Adjust your diet accordingly based on the your results. Consider tracking your diet more frequently if you find it far off your goals.

Endurance

Endurance is the first of three training steps to a faster 10K and improved performance. It is the cornerstone on which the other two training steps, Strength and Speed, are built.

Although the endurance stage of training may be the easiest to attain, it is also the most important. Without a solid foundation of at least 3-5 weeks of Endurance training, Strength or Speed training will offer minimal returns in improved performance, and may in fact lead to injury.

Learn to run relaxed

Master the art of running relaxed during your endurance training runs: (1) keep your wrists and hands loose; (2) run with your thumbs up and elbows in, close to your side, to prevent your arms from tightening up; (3) relax your lower jaw; feel it move up and down with each stride, and; (4) run "tall" with your hips sightly forward, without any forward lean; keep your feet under your body as you maintain a good stride.

Set your training distance

As a general rule, run your shorter Endurance runs at about 75% of your event distance and your longer Endurance runs at about 125% of event distance. For example, if training for a 10K (6.2 miles) race, your shorter Endurance runs would be 4-5 miles, and your longer ones 7-9 miles.

Adjust your training distances to your fitness level as it changes throughout your training season. Run shorter distances early in the season, and longer distances as you make progress with your training. Limit your mileage increases to less than 10% per week to prevent injury.

Alternate your long runs with medium or short runs to help your body recover from previous day's training, and to keep you fresh mentally and physically.

Set your training pace

Set your training pace to be able to maintain it throughout your run. Find a pace that allows you to run loose and tall. Adjust your pace to your fitness level as it changes throughout your training season; a pace that is too fast at the beginning of the season may be too slow at the end of the season.

Remember that in Endurance training pace is less important than distance.

Run your slow Endurance runs at about 50% of race pace, your medium Endurance runs at about 70% of race pace and your fast Endurance runs at about 85% of race pace.

Mix up your courses

Incorporate different courses into your Endurance training. Find at least five different courses to mix into your running routine to keep you mentally and physically fresh.

Choose a variety of running surfaces to help prevent injury. Find routes that take you on grass, sand or dirt trails as alternates to running every day on cement sidewalks or asphalt roads.

Be creative in designing your courses. Include loop, out-and-back, and point-to-point runs. Mix in courses with hills, gentle slopes, scenery, curves, straights, and flats. Have fun!

Sample week of Endurance training

Here is an example of how to put together a week of training to focus on Endurance:

Monday: *Run a short, easy run. Stay relaxed and comfortable.*
Tuesday: *Run a medium distance run. Remember to run tall and relaxed.*
Wednesday: *Run a long distance run. Run slowly. Stay loose and smooth. Enjoy the scenery along the way.*
Thursday: *Run medium distance. Get in the groove and lose yourself in the run.*
Friday: *Do a long, slow run. Don't worry about pace. Try to go an extra mile or two.*
Saturday: *Go on a short run. Stay loose and enjoy it.*
Sunday: *Day off. Let your body recover and rejuvenate itself.*

Running for strength

Running for Strength is the second training step to a faster 10K and increased performance. It bridges the training gap between Endurance and Speed work. Build a base of at least 3-5 weeks of Endurance training before mixing Strength workouts into your training.

The two types of running for strength workouts are: (1) Hills and Stairs, and (2) Fartleks.

Run Hills and Stairs to build power

Strength training improves your running by putting power and strength into your stride. This added power in your stride will help you slide through training runs and help you run relaxed during races. The runners who incorporate running strength workouts into their training will always beat the runners who run only for endurance.

Running Hills and Stairs will build power into your upper legs. This power provides you the strength to lengthen your stride and get more distance with every step.

Maintain your form on Hills and Stairs

Concentrate on good running form, more than pace, to get the most out of running Hills and Stairs Remember, this is Strength work, not Speed work (you'll do that later, on the track).

Set your pace so that you'll be tired at the end of the workout, but not exhausted.

Concentrate on good running form. Visualize it: Drive your knees up and pump your arms on every stride; run tall and drive off the balls of your feet. Adjust your running form to meet the hill: shorten your stride; increase your tempo.

Choose your Hills and Stairs from what is available

You can run Hills and Stairs two ways: (1) Hill or Stair Repeats, and (2) Hill Circuits. Choose the workouts according to what options you have available to you. Mix up your Hill and Stair workouts to keep you fresh and to prevent injury.

Sample Hill and Stair workouts

Here are examples of Hill and Stair workouts. Use these as guidelines for your workouts. Adjust your runs to your fitness level as it changes throughout your training.

Hill Repeats

(1) Find a hill with approximately 15% gradient, almost as steep as a flight of stairs in your home. (2) Warm up with a 1 to 2 mile easy run. (3) Run 300 meters

up the hill. Remember to focus on good running form, not speed. (4) Walk or jog slowly down the hill to prevent knee injury. (5) Repeat 8-12 times. (6) Cool down with a 1-2 mile easy run.

Stairs

(1) Find a nearby school with a stadium or a set of outdoor stairs that can accommodate your workouts. (2) Run to the top of the stairs. Again, concentrate on your running form, not pace; keep your knees up and pump your arms. (3) Be careful as you walk or jog down the stairs. (4) Repeat for a 15-minute set. (The number of runs you do to the top of the stairs in that time will depend on the height of the stairs.)

Hill Circuits

(1) Find a medium distance run that includes a series of several hills. (2) Design your course to take you through at least 1-2 miles of flat terrain as a warm up before you come to any hills. (3) Run up and jog down your first hill, then move on the next one. (4) Repeat 7-10 hills. (5) Include a 1-2 mile warm down after the hills. Find a course you can use repeatedly.

Run Fartleks for Strength

Fartleks are the second type of running strength workouts. Fartleks are training runs that include periods of hard then easy intervals in a continuous run. They will give you the strength to accelerate as needed to adjust to pace changes in a race. Fartleks also teach your body tempo and rhythm.

Concentrate on running tall, smooth and strong during the hard Fartlek intervals. Accelerate to 75-80% of your race pace. Remember that this is Strength work, not Speed work, so don't sprint or race. Control and maintain this moderately fast pace.

Focus on running relaxed, slowly and loose on the easy Fartlek intervals. Run as slowly as 30% of your race pace. Catch your breath with long, slow deep breaths and recover fully in preparation for the next hard interval. Shorten your slow/recovery intervals as you move through your training season, and improve your conditioning.

Sample Fartlek workouts

Use the following examples of Fartlek workouts as guidelines of how to build strength into your stride and to put a bounce into your step.

2-Minute Fartlek

(1) Find an easy, open course. (2) Warm up with an easy 1 mile run. (3) While running, accelerate into a 2-minute hard run; control the pace and run smooth. (4) Run 2 minutes easy; recover and run loose. (5) Repeat this hard/easy Fartlek for 30 minutes. (6) Warm down with a 1 mile easy run.

Pyramid Fartlek

(1) Find an easy, open course. (2) Warm up with a 1 mile easy run. (3) Run 15

seconds hard, followed by 15 seconds easy. (5) Then run 30 seconds hard, followed by 30 seconds easy. (6) Increase by 15 seconds each hard/easy interval, until you reach 2-minute intervals.

When your training level allows, follow this back down from 2 minute intervals to 15 second intervals.

(7) Warm down with an easy 1 mile run.

Sample week of Running for Strength

Here is a sample week of training which shows how to incorporate Strength runs with your Endurance runs:

Monday: *Go on a long distance run. Relax, stay comfortable and enjoy it.*
Tuesday: *Run a medium Hill Circuit run, about 90-100% of race distance. Maintain form up the hills and run strong.*
Wednesday: *Do a short run. Stay loose. Let your body recover and rejuvenate.*
Thursday: *Do a 2-Minute Fartlek run. Remember to run tall and smooth.*
Friday: *Run long and easy. Lose yourself in the run and stay relaxed.*
Saturday: *Run 10-15 minutes of Stairs, followed by a very short run of no more than 40-50% of race distance.*
Sunday: *Day off. Give your body a chance to rest and recover.*

Speed work

Speed work is the third and final training step to a faster 10K and increased performance. You'll put the finishing touches on your Endurance and Strength workouts with 3-5 weeks of Speed training. Speed work will give you an extra gear into which you can shift during spirited training or races.

Build a training base before Speed work

Although Speed work can give a runner the ability to mass-produce personal records, it is also the cause of most injuries. Consider doing Speed work only after building a training foundation of Endurance and Strength. Only with this foundation can Speed work be effective and safe.

Warm up before speed work

Warm up and stretch thoroughly before running any Speed work to prevent injuries and increase your performance. Run at least 1-2 miles easy as warm up. Pay special attention to your stretching before Speed work, even though you may not stretch much before Endurance runs. (See the Stretching tip in this guide.)

Set your Speed work distances

Teach your body to run faster for a given race distance by giving it a distance at which it can run faster than your current race pace.

Set your Speed work distances according to your race distance. Run longer intervals when training for longer races. Run shorter intervals for shorter ones. Run intervals of 200 meters, 400 meters and 800 meters and 1 mile for races of 10k (6.2 miles) or less.

Decrease the length and increase the pace of your intervals as your conditioning improves through your training season and your race date nears. Run shorter, faster intervals 2-3 weeks prior to your race to help you peak.

Set your Speed work intervals

As a general rule, run your intervals at a pace faster than your race pace. This teaches your body that it can run faster than your race pace. But the key to getting the most out of your Speed work is to run your intervals at just the right amount faster than race pace. Running too fast will lead to injury and not fast enough will limit improvement.

Run mile intervals 3-5% faster than race pace. Run 1/2 mile and 1/4 mile intervals 8-12% faster than race pace. And run 1/8 mile intervals 12-15% faster than race race.

For example, if you run a 40:00 10K, this is a 6:22 race pace per mile. You would run your mile intervals at 6:00-6:10, your 800 meter (1/2 mile) intervals at 2:50-2:55, your 400 meter (1/4 mile) intervals at 1:25-1:30 and 200 meter (1/8 mile) intervals at :38-:42.

Adjust your interval pace to your conditioning level as it changes throughout your training season. Refer to the Interval Pace Chart in this guide to find your interval pace.

Run your intervals hard, but controlled.

Set your recovery
Set your recovery times and distances so you can maintain consistent times throughout your workout, but not long enough for you to get cold between intervals.

Walk or jog half the distance of the interval being run as a general rule for recovery. Limit your recovery to less than 5:00 minutes to prevent cool down.

Sample Speed Workouts
Use the following Speed workouts as examples of how to build your own Speed workouts:

Mile intervals
(1) Stretch and warm up completely with an easy 1-mile run. (2) Run 4x1-mile intervals at 3-5% faster than race pace. (3) Walk/jog 400 meters (1/4 mile) between intervals. Maintain consistent interval times and rest between intervals. (4) Warm down with an easy 1-mile run.

Remember to adjust your interval and recovery times according to your fitness level as it changes throughout your training season.

800 meter intervals
(1) Stretch and warm up completely with an easy 1-mile run. (2) Run 6x800 meter (1/2 mile) intervals at 8-10% faster than race pace. Maintain consistent interval times and rest between intervals. (3) Walk/jog 200 or 400 meters (1/8-1/4 mile) between intervals (depending on how hard you run the intervals). Maintain consistent interval times and rest between intervals. (4) Warm down with an easy 1-mile run.

Remember to adjust your interval and recovery times according to your fitness level as it changes throughout your training season.

400 meter intervals
(1) Stretch and warm up completely with an easy 1-mile run. (2) Run 3 sets of 4x400 meter (1/4 mile) intervals (a total of 12x400's) at 10-12% faster than race pace. (3) Walk/jog 200 meters (1/8 mile) between intervals, and rest 5:00 minutes between sets. (4) Warm down with an easy 1-mile run.

Remember to adjust your interval and recovery times according to your fitness level as it changes throughout your training season.

400/200 meter intervals

(1) Stretch and warm up completely with an easy 1-mile run. (2) Run 400 meters at race pace. (3) Walk/jog 200 meter recovery. (4) Run 200 meters at 12-15% faster than race pace. (5) Rest for 4:00 minute recovery. (6) Repeat four times (for total of 4x400 and 4x200 intervals). (7) Warm down with a 1 mile easy run.

Remember to adjust your interval and recovery times according to your fitness level as it changes throughout your training season.

200 meter intervals

(1) Stretch and warm up completely with an easy 1-mile run. (2) Run 4x200 meter intervals at 12-15% faster than race pace, with a 30 second recovery between intervals. (3) Rest 4:00 between sets of 4x200. (4) Repeat set four times (for total of 12x200 meters). (5) Warm down with an easy 1 mile run.

Remember to adjust your interval and recovery times according to your fitness level as it changes throughout your training season.

Negative split intervals

(1) Stretch and warm up completely with an easy 1-mile run. (2) Run 1 mile at 3-5% faster than race pace. (3) Walk/jog 400 meter recovery. (4) Run 1200 meters (3/4 mile) at 5-7% faster than race pace. (5) Walk/jog 400 meter recovery. (6) Run 800 meters (1/2 mile) at 8-10% faster than race pace. (7) Walk/jog 400 meter recovery. (8) Run 400 meters (1/4 mile) at 10-12% faster than race pace. Concentrate on running each interval at a faster pace than the previous interval. (9) Run an easy 1 mile warm down.

Sample week of Speed work

Here is a sample week to show how to incorporate Endurance, Strength and Speed workouts.

Monday: *Do a medium distance run about 80-100% of race distance. Relax and run a smooth, controlled pace.*

Tuesday: *Run 4 1-mile intervals. Keep interval times as consistent as possible.*

Wednesday: *Run a short distance run of 50-75% of race distance. Relax and recover from previous day's workout.*

Thursday: *Run Pyramid Fartlek workout (:15 hard/:15 easy; :30 hard/:30 easy, up to 2:00 hard/2:00 easy, and back down).*

Friday: *Run medium distance run of 80-100% race distance. Maintain strong pace, good form and run tall.*

Saturday: *Run long, slow distance of 125-150% of race distance. Run smooth and relaxed. Enjoy the scenery along the way.*

Sunday: *Day off, or short run of no more than 25-50% of race distance, easy! Let your body recover and rejuvenate from the week.*

Surviving running injuries

The joy of running can be matched in intensity only with the agony of a running injury that prevents you from running. Don't let the terrific progress you've made in your training program be derailed by a running injury. Use these suggestions to (1) *prevent* injuries from hindering you in the first place, and (2) *minimize* the effect they have on your training and racing.

Prevention is the best cure

Clearly the best way to survive a running injury is to avoid it in the first place. Avoid running injuries by following these reminders.

Stretch and warm up completely

Stretch before and after each run. This is the simplest step you can take to prevent injury. Refer to the stretching tip in this guide for specific stretches to help you.

Ease into your runs. Design your courses to allow you at least 1 mile of easy warm up before you settle into your workout's focused pace. This is the second simplest step to prevent injury. Just start out slowly!

Mix up your workouts

Most running injuries are caused by repeating too often the same workouts over and over again. Mix up your workouts: (1) Vary your distance; alternate short, medium and long runs into your running week. (2) Change your pace; run easy on some days, medium on others and hard on some others depending on your workout focus. (3) Run on different terrain; mix in runs on dirt trails, grass or sand with your runs on cement sidewalks and asphalt roads. (4) Build your running distance and intensity slowly over many weeks or months to give your body time to recover during building periods.

Cross train

Cross training is an extension of the idea of mixing up your workouts. Only in cross training, instead of mixing up your running workouts with other types of running workouts, you mix them up with other sports: cycling, rowing, cross country skiing, walking, swimming, or weightlifting.

Cross train to help prevent running injuries by (1) giving your body a break from repeatedly doing the same movement, action and pounding of running, and (2) by strengthening your body in ways that complement your running-developed muscles.

Keep your shoes fit

Running shoes are the most critical pieces of equipment to a runner. Take the time to try on and test run several brands to find the one that fits you best. Then stick with the brand and style that works best for you. Look for annual shoe-buying guides in running magazines for information on new models and changes.

Don't skimp on your shoes. Plan on spending at least $60 for a good pair of shoes. To prevent injury from your shoes losing absorption qualities or developing worn surfaces, replace them at least every 500 miles (that's only 4 months of 25 miles per week!) or earlier as needed.

Minimize the damage after it's done

The goal is to try to prevent injuries. But if it's too late, here are some ideas to help you survive your running injury:

Find an acceptable way to rest

If it hurts when you run, then you need to limit your running or stop entirely to give your body a chance to recuperate. To help you survive this rest, determine if all running hurts you, or only certain running. If it hurts only when you run hills, then cut that out of your training. Or if medium or hard runs hurt, then try easy runs. This may help you retain your sanity through your rest. Be aware of what training hurts you so you can avoid it before damage occurs. Review your training diary to find the training that caused the injury.

If all running hurts, consider other training, such as swimming, cycling, rowing, cross country skiing or weight training. This should limit the overall loss of fitness during your recovery while giving your injury the time to heal.

Ice and heat to get by

When you're not entirely sidelined by your injury, you may be able to use ice and heat to let you continue training. Hold an ice pack against the spot of the injury immediately after working out to limit swelling like knee injuries, shin splints and ankle sprains. Use heat on the point of an injury to increase circulation to the area on injuries such as back sciatica.

Use your diary to identify the problem

Your training diary is often your most effective diagnostic tool to help you identify the cause of your injuries. Refer to your diary to see if an increase in distance or in strength or speed work precipitated your first injury symptoms. Maybe a particular type of terrain on a run was the last run prior to the injury.

Use the diary to give you answers to your training and racing questions. Then, adjust your training to reduce, minimize or eliminate the problem.

Fun runs and overtraining

Fun runs

Mix up your workouts to prevent boredom and injury. Here are some course ideas to keep your runs interesting and fresh:

Point-to-point runs

Run from point A to point B, and have a friend or coach pick you up at point B to drive you back to point A. Think of new ways to incorporate point-to-point runs.

Scenic runs

Drive to a scenic area such as the beach, lake front or mountains to find a scenic run that is as good for your soul as it is for your body.

Trail runs

Find a quiet running trail that takes you through the rolling hills as a way to forget the consistency of always running the straight and narrow road.

Follow the leader

With a friend or two or more, play follow the leader on a run in whichever direction the leader chooses.

Exploratory runs

Take the time to pick a new road, a new direction, or a new path to follow for an exploratory run.

Have fun. Be creative!

Overtraining

Overtraining is the point where your training and daily stresses add up to over-tax your system. A training program that may not be overtraining one week may be overtraining the next because of additional stresses at work or elsewhere. Be aware of possible overtraining as you: (1) increase your training level, or (2) experience a major change in your personal life.

Watch for signs of overtraining

Watch for a high resting pulse rate when you first wake. Beware if you you have trouble falling asleep, sleeping or if you feel tired all the time. Consider overtraining as a cause of becoming upset more easily with everyday situations.

Cure overtraining

Back off your training if you think you may be overtraining. Take a couple of days off, reduce the intensity of your training, and get more rest.

Trim the "training fat" from your workout schedule. Concentrate on quality not quantity. Don't overtrain. Train well, race well, have fun, and feel great.

Other Books to Read

Run Log's training guide offers tips and workouts to help you get more out of your training. Refer to these books for more in depth discussions of other training and racing topics:

Running Racing and Training
Fixx, James: *The Complete Book of Running*, Random House
Henderson, Joe: *Running Your Best Race*, W.C. Brown
Lynch, Jerry: *The Total Runner*, Prentice Hall

Cross-Training
Allen, Mark and Babbit, Bob: *Mark Allen's Total Triathlete*, Contemporary Books
Bass, Jan and Houts, Tim: *Tri Log, Training Diary and Guide for the Triathlete*, Sports Log Publishers
Doughty, Tom: *The Complete Book of Long Distance and Competitive Cycling*, Simon & Schuster
Prins, Jan: *The Illustrated Swimmer*, Honolulu He'e
Scott, Dave and Barrett, Liz: *Dave Scott's Triathlon Training*, Simon & Schuster
Vaz, Katherine: *Cross Training, The Complete Book of the Triathlon*, Avon Publishers

Nutrition
Brody, Jane: *Jane Brody's Good Food Book*, Bantam Books
Haas, Robert: *Eat to Win*, Rawson Associates
Kraus, Barbera: *Calories and Carbohydrates*, Grosset & Dunlap
The Complete & Up-to-Date Fat Book, a guide to the fat, calories and fat percentages in your food, Avery Publishing Group

Periodicals
Bicycling, 33 E. Minor St., Emmaus, PA 18098
Running Times, 18 Azailia Ave., Fairfax, CA 94930
Runners World, 33 E. Minor St., Emmaus, PA 18098
Triathlete, 1127 Hamilton St., Allentown, PA 18102

Getting more out of your diary

Use the training diary as a tool to help you get more out of your training. *Run Log's* diary pages are simple and roomy to give you plenty of space and flexibility to decide what and how much information to record.

The diary can help keep you honest to your workout goals (like a personal coach does) by reminding you of what you have or haven't done. It can also provide a wealth of information to review when you need to find out why you did so well, or not-so-well in a particular event.

Use these suggestions (in addition to the course, distance and notes hightlighted on the diary pages) as guidelines to help you get more out of your training diary:

Note Days Off
Draw a diagonal line through the entire day's diary section to show a day off from training. Days off are critical to a good training program. But too many days off will erode your training. Note why you took the day off, whether for rest, injury, or boredom. This will keep you honest or point to a need to change your schedule.

Adjust your notes to your changing needs through your season
Remember that the Run Log diary allows you the flexibility to decide what training information is important, *to you*, to record. This information may change through the year as you focus on different goals. For example, at the beginning of the year you may record your weight on a daily basis to help you focus on returning to your ideal race weight. While in mid-season you may note your weight only once a week and note your pace per mile each run.

Adjust your regular entries to your training goals as they change through the season.

Note what you feel
How many miles and how many minutes you run are important *objective* data to record each day. Equally important, and why *Run Log* is called a training *diary*, is the *subjective* data of how you feel during and after your training. Remember that day-to-day non-training demands (i.e. job, family or relationship stresses) impact your running as much as your training does.

Take advantage of the extra space provided in the *Run Log* diary to note thoughts about both training and non-training events.

How to use charts

We've included five charts to help you better plan and track your training. Here's a summary of these charts and how to use them.

Training & Race Pace Chart

This chart lets you determine: (1) your pace needed to finish a given training or race distance in a projected time, (2) your total time for a given training or race distance, and (3) your 1/4 mile race pace from your race finish time.

Calculate your race pace goal

To calculate the average pace to finish in a given time: (1) find the desired finish time in the appropriate *distance* column and (2) find the associated pace in the *pace/mile* column. For example, if you want to finish a 10K in 40:23, you need to average 6:30 per mile. Use this per mile pace during a race to help you judge at each mile mark whether or not you're on pace for your goal finish time.

Calculate your finish time goal

To calculate your total time for a given training or race distance based on a goal per mile average: (1) find the pace per mile in the *pace/mile* column, and (2) find the associated total time in the *distance* column. Use this total time to help you determine if you're running your endurance runs at the right pace.

Calculate your 1/4 mile pace

To find your 1/4 mile interval race pace: (1) locate your race finish time in the appropriate *distance* column and (2) find the associated 1/4 mile pace in the *pace per 1/4 mile* column. Use this 1/4 mile pace with the Interval Pace Chart in this guide to plan your interval training.

Interval Training Pace Chart

This chart will help you set your goal Speed training intervals.

To find your goal Speed training intervals: (1) Find your 1/4 mile race pace on the Training and Race Pace Chart; (2) Find your 1/4 mile race pace in the *pace per 1/4 mile* column; (3) Use the associated interval times from the appropriate *1/8 mile, 1/4 mile, 1/2 mile or 1 mile* columns.

Each interval distance shows a range of interval goal times. Use these as guidelines for your intervals; adjust your interval times to your conditioning as it changes throughout your training season.

Map to Raceday Worksheet

This worksheet will help you plan a multi-week training program for a specific event.

To plan your training for a specific event: (1) mark week #1 or #2 as your training peak for your event (1 or 2 weeks prior to the event); (2) mark the week number that you will begin your training; (3) plan each week's training in a schedule that will allow you to build gradually from your training start point to your training peak. Never increase mileage more than 10% per week. Allow time to stay at "training plateaus" before moving on to subsequent stages of training.

Race Results Summary

The Race Results Summary lets you put in one place all of your race results. Remember to note any comments about the race or conditions that affected your results. Review this page against your training prior to races to learn what training works best for you.

Cumulative Mileage Chart

This chart lets you graph your training mileage. There are 28 vertical lines on two pages allowing you to graph 13 months of training. Mark the week along the bottom of the chart and graph your weekly mileage to the corresponding distance level. Review your race results against your weekly training distances.

Training & Race Pace Chart

pace/ mile	pace/ 1/4 mile	5k	8k*	10k	15k	10mi	13.1mi	25k	26.2mi
4:30	1:08	13:59	22:22	27:58	41:57	45:00	58:57	1:09:54	1:57:54
4:40	1:10	14:30	23:12	29:00	43:30	46:40	1:01:08	1:12:30	2:02:16
4:50	1:12	15:01	24:02	30:02	45:03	48:20	1:03:19	1:15:05	2:06:38
5:00	1:15	15:32	24:51	31:04	46:36	50:00	1:05:30	1:17:40	2:11:00
5:10	1:18	16:03	25:41	32:06	48:09	51:40	1:07:41	1:20:16	2:15:22
5:20	1:20	16:34	26:31	33:08	49:43	53:20	1:09:52	1:22:51	2:19:44
5:30	1:22	17:05	27:20	34:11	51:16	55:00	1:12:03	1:25:26	2:24:06
5:40	1:25	17:36	28:10	35:13	52:49	56:40	1:14:14	1:28:02	2:28:28
5:50	1:28	18:07	29:00	36:15	54:22	58:20	1:16:25	1:30:37	2:32:50
6:00	1:30	18:38	29:50	37:17	55:55	1:00:00	1:18:36	1:33:12	2:37:12
6:10	1:32	19:10	30:39	38:19	57:29	1:01:40	1:20:47	1:35:48	2:41:34
6:20	1:35	19:41	31:29	39:21	59:02	1:03:20	1:22:58	1:38:23	2:45:56
6:30	1:38	20:12	32:19	40:23	1:00:35	1:05:00	1:25:09	1:40:58	2:50:18
6:40	1:40	20:43	33:08	41:25	1:02:08	1:06:40	1:27:20	1:43:34	2:54:40
6:50	1:42	21:14	33:58	42:28	1:03:41	1:08:20	1:29:31	1:46:09	2:59:02
7:00	1:45	21:45	34:48	43:30	1:05:15	1:10:00	1:31:42	1:48:44	3:03:24
7:10	1:48	22:16	35:38	44:32	1:06:48	1:11:40	1:33:53	1:51:20	3:07:46
7:20	1:50	22:47	36:27	45:34	1:08:21	1:13:20	1:36:04	1:53:55	3:12:08
7:30	1:52	23:18	37:17	46:36	1:09:54	1:15:00	1:38:15	1:56:30	3:16:30
7:40	1:55	23:49	38:07	47:38	1:11:27	1:16:40	1:40:26	1:59:06	3:20:52
7:50	1:58	24:20	38:56	48:40	1:13:01	1:18:20	1:42:37	2:01:41	3:25:14
8:00	2:00	24:51	39:46	49:43	1:14:34	1:20:00	1:44:48	2:04:16	3:29:36
8:10	2:02	25:22	40:36	50:45	1:16:07	1:21:40	1:46:59	2:06:52	3:33:58
8:20	2:05	25:53	41:25	51:47	1:17:40	1:23:20	1:49:10	2:09:27	3:38:20
8:30	2:08	26:24	42:15	52:49	1:19:13	1:25:00	1:51:21	2:12:02	3:42:42
8:40	2:10	26:56	43:05	53:51	1:20:47	1:26:40	1:53:32	2:14:38	3:47:04
8:50	2:12	27:27	43:55	54:53	1:22:20	1:28:20	1:55:43	2:17:13	3:51:26
9:00	2:15	27:58	44:44	55:55	1:23:53	1:30:00	1:57:54	2:19:49	3:55:48
9:10	2:18	28:29	45:34	56:58	1:25:26	1:31:40	2:00:05	2:22:24	4:00:10
9:20	2:20	29:00	46:24	58:00	1:27:00	1:33:20	2:02:16	2:24:59	4:04:32
9:30	2:22	29:31	47:13	59:02	1:28:33	1:35:00	2:04:27	2:27:35	4:08:54
9:40	2:25	30:02	48:03	1:00:04	1:30:06	1:36:40	2:06:38	2:30:10	4:13:16
9:50	2:28	30:33	48:53	1:01:06	1:31:39	1:38:20	2:08:49	2:32:45	4:17:38

* Use 8k distance as an equivalent to 5 miles since 8k equals 4.97 miles.

Interval Training Pace Chart

pace per 1/4 mile	1/8 mile 112%	115%	1/4 mile 108%	112%	1/2 mile 108%	110%	1 mile 103%	105%
1:08	:30	:29	1:02	:59	2:04	2:01	4:22	4:17
1:10	:31	:30	1:04	1:02	2:09	2:06	4:32	4:26
1:12	:32	:31	1:07	1:04	2:13	2:10	4:41	4:36
1:15	:33	:32	1:09	1:06	2:18	2:15	4:51	4:45
1:18	:34	33	1:11	1:08	2:23	2:19	5:01	4:55
1:20	:35	:34	1:14	1:10	2:27	2:24	5:10	5:04
1:22	:36	:35	1:16	1:13	2:32	2:28	5:20	5:14
1:25	:37	:36	1:18	1:15	2:36	2:33	5:30	5:23
1:28	:39	37	1:20	1:17	2:41	2:38	5:39	5:33
1:30	:40	:38	1:23	1:19	2:46	2:42	5:49	5:42
1:32	:41	:39	1:25	1:21	2:50	2:47	5:59	5:51
1:35	:42	:40	1:27	1:24	2:55	2:51	6:09	6:01
1:38	:43	:41	1:30	1:26	2:59	2:56	6:18	6:10
1:40	:44	:42	1:32	1:28	3:04	3:00	6:28	6:20
1:42	:45	:44	1:34	1:30	3:09	3:05	6:38	6:29
1:45	:46	:45	1:37	1:32	3:13	3:09	6:47	6:39
1:48	:47	:46	1:39	1:35	3:18	3:14	6:57	6:48
1:50	:48	:47	1:41	1:37	3:22	3:18	7:07	6:58
1:52	:49	:48	1:43	1:39	3:27	3:22	7:16	7:07
1:55	:51	:49	1:46	1:41	3:32	3:27	7:26	7:17
1:58	:52	:50	1:48	1:43	3:36	3:31	7:36	7:26
2:00	:53	:51	1:50	1:46	3:41	3:36	7:46	7:36
2:02	:54	:52	1:53	1:48	3:45	3:40	7:55	7:46
2:05	:55	:53	1:55	1:50	3:50	3:45	8:05	7:55
2:08	:56	:54	1:57	1:52	3:55	3:49	8:15	8:05
2:10	:57	:55	2:00	1:54	3:59	3:54	8:24	8:14
2:12	:58	:56	2:02	1:57	4:04	3:58	8:34	8:24
2:15	:59	:57	2:04	1:59	4:08	4:03	8:44	8:33
2:18	1:00	:58	2:07	2:01	4:13	4:08	8:54	8:43
2:20	1:02	:59	2:09	2:03	4:18	4:12	9:03	8:52
2:22	1:03	1:01	2:11	2:05	4:22	4:17	9:13	9:02
2:25	1:04	1:02	2:13	2:08	4:27	4:21	9:23	9:11
2:28	1:05	1:03	2:16	2:10	4:31	4:26	9:32	9:21

Map to Raceday Worksheet

	MON.	TUES.	WED.	THUR.	FRI.	SAT.	SUN.	TOTAL
WEEK #17	Type:____ Miles:____	Type:____ Miles:____	Type:____ Miles:____	Type:____ Miles:____	Type:____ Miles:____	Type:____ Miles:____	Type:____ Miles:____	Miles:____
WEEK #16	Type:____ Miles:____	Type:____ Miles:____	Type:____ Miles:____	Type:____ Miles:____	Type:____ Miles:____	Type:____ Miles:____	Type:____ Miles:____	Miles:____
WEEK #15	Type:____ Miles:____	Type:____ Miles:____	Type:____ Miles:____	Type:____ Miles:____	Type:____ Miles:____	Type:____ Miles:____	Type:____ Miles:____	Miles:____
WEEK #14	Type:____ Miles:____	Type:____ Miles:____	Type:____ Miles:____	Type:____ Miles:____	Type:____ Miles:____	Type:____ Miles:____	Type:____ Miles:____	Miles:____
WEEK #13	Type:____ Miles:____	Type:____ Miles:____	Type:____ Miles:____	Type:____ Miles:____	Type:____ Miles:____	Type:____ Miles:____	Type:____ Miles:____	Miles:____
WEEK #12	Type:____ Miles:____	Type:____ Miles:____	Type:____ Miles:____	Type:____ Miles:____	Type:____ Miles:____	Type:____ Miles:____	Type:____ Miles:____	Miles:____

21

Map to Raceday Worksheet

	MON.	TUES.	WED.	THUR.	FRI.	SAT.	SUN.	TOTAL
WEEK #11	Type:___ Miles:___	Type:___ Miles:___	Type:___ Miles:___	Type:___ Miles:___	Type:___ Miles:___	Type:___ Miles:___	Type:___ Miles:___	Miles:___
WEEK #10	Type:___ Miles:___	Type:___ Miles:___	Type:___ Miles:___	Type:___ Miles:___	Type:___ Miles:___	Type:___ Miles:___	Type:___ Miles:___	Miles:___
WEEK #9	Type:___ Miles:___	Type:___ Miles:___	Type:___ Miles:___	Type:___ Miles:___	Type:___ Miles:___	Type:___ Miles:___	Type:___ Miles:___	Miles:___
WEEK #8	Type:___ Miles:___	Type:___ Miles:___	Type:___ Miles:___	Type:___ Miles:___	Type:___ Miles:___	Type:___ Miles:___	Type:___ Miles:___	Miles:___
WEEK #7	Type:___ Miles:___	Type:___ Miles:___	Type:___ Miles:___	Type:___ Miles:___	Type:___ Miles:___	Type:___ Miles:___	Type:___ Miles:___	Miles:___
WEEK #6	Type:___ Miles:___	Type:___ Miles:___	Type:___ Miles:___	Type:___ Miles:___	Type:___ Miles:___	Type:___ Miles:___	Type:___ Miles:___	Miles:___

Map to Raceday Worksheet

	MON.	TUES.	WED.	THUR.	FRI.	SAT.	SUN.	TOTAL
WEEK #5	Type:___ Miles:___	Type:___ Miles:___	Type:___ Miles:___	Type:___ Miles:___	Type:___ Miles:___	Type:___ Miles:___	Type:___ Miles:___	Miles:___
WEEK #4	Type:___ Miles:___	Type:___ Miles:___	Type:___ Miles:___	Type:___ Miles:___	Type:___ Miles:___	Type:___ Miles:___	Type:___ Miles:___	Miles:___
WEEK #3	Type:___ Miles:___	Type:___ Miles:___	Type:___ Miles:___	Type:___ Miles:___	Type:___ Miles:___	Type:___ Miles:___	Type:___ Miles:___	Miles:___
WEEK #2	Type:___ Miles:___	Type:___ Miles:___	Type:___ Miles:___	Type:___ Miles:___	Type:___ Miles:___	Type:___ Miles:___	Type:___ Miles:___	Miles:___
WEEK #1	Type:___ Miles:___	Type:___ Miles:___	Type:___ Miles:___	Type:___ Miles:___	Type:___ Miles:___	Type:___ Miles:___	Type:___ Miles:___	Miles:___
RACEWEEK	Type:___ Miles:___	Type:___ Miles:___	Type:___ Miles:___	Type:___ Miles:___	Type:___ Miles:___	Type:___ Miles:___	Type:___ Miles:___	Miles:___

Race Results Summary

Event	Course description and comments	Distance	Time	Avg. Pace

Race Results Summary

Event	Course description and comments	Distance	Time	Avg. Pace

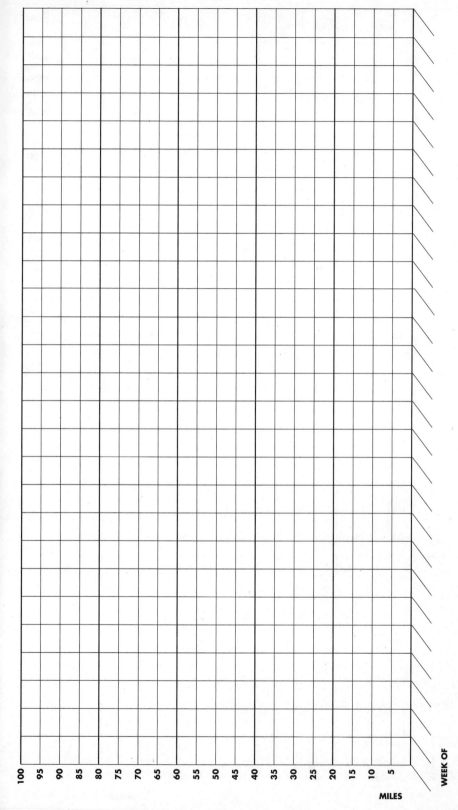

CUMULATIVE **MILEAGE CHART**

100
95
90
85
80
75
70
65
60
55
50
45
40
35
30
25
20
15
10
5

MILES

WEEK OF

CUMULATIVE **MILEAGE CHART**

| 100 |
| 95 |
| 90 |
| 85 |
| 80 |
| 75 |
| 70 |
| 65 |
| 60 |
| 55 |
| 50 |
| 45 |
| 40 |
| 35 |
| 30 |
| 25 |
| 20 |
| 15 |
| 10 |
| 5 |

MILES

WEEK OF

Above: The second leg begins in the high school 4 x 100 meter relay, 1993 Penn Relays, Philadelphia, Pennsylvania. Previous page: Willie Mtola catches and passes Andre Espinoza to win the 1992 New York Marathon.

"Let him that would move the world, first move himself."

-Socrates

MON.

Saucony Shadow 706.1 km
Asics 123   488.75
Saucony Jazz   46.35
Asics 125   0

DATE Dec 30 96

COURSE/NOTES _____
_____ Saucony Shadow II 0 _____
_____ Asics Gel Racer 7 races _____
_____
_____

7°C @ 0743 Raining   slept 6 hours   MILES/TIME

TUES.

DATE Dec 31 96

COURSE/NOTES _____
_____
_____
_____
_____
_____

5°C @ 0755 Overcast slept 7½ hours   MILES/TIME 1175.1 km
                                                  for 1996

WED.

DATE Jan 1 1997

COURSE/NOTES _____
_____
_____
_____
_____

9°C @ 1336   Overcast Slept 8 hours MILES/TIME

THUR.

DATE Jan 2, 1997

COURSE/NOTES _____
_____
_____
_____
_____

7.5°C @ 0806 Overcast Slept 8½ hours MILES/TIME

DATE Jan.3, 97   **F**RI.

COURSE/NOTES _____
_____
_____
_____

Later in day a weak voice
Feel tired like I have a head cold
1°C @ 0724   Mostly clear   Slept 6 hours   MILES/TIME [   ] km

DATE Jan.4, 97   **S**AT.

COURSE/NOTES   Cycle with Bruce Law _____
_____
_____
_____

head cold symptoms
Feel tired, little energy, weak voice runny nose
3.5°C @ 0848   Overcast   Slept 7½ hours   MILES/TIME [21 K]

DATE Jan.5 97   **S**UN.

COURSE/NOTES _____
_____
_____
_____

Feel tired, low energy, lots of sputum
-0.5°C @ 0812   Slept 7½ hours   MILES/TIME [   ]

                                                           REVIEW

GOALS/NOTES _____
_____
_____
_____
_____

WEIGHT [   ]   CUMULATIVE   [   ]   WEEKLY   [   ]
                         TOTAL   TOTAL

                        cycle 21 M

MON.

COURSE/NOTES _____

still have cold symptoms
7°C @ 0640 (B) Raining   slept 7 1/4 hours   MILES/TIME

TUES.

COURSE/NOTES _____

Still have a cold a fairly bad cold
Feel very tired run down   lots of sputum
5°C @ 0800 (B) Overcast   slept 9 1/2 hours   MILES/TIME

WED.

COURSE/NOTES _____

coughing a little tight chest
very tired feeling like I have very little energy
still have a definite cold   lots of sputum
4°C on radio
5°C @ 0733 (B) Overcast   slept 8 1/2 hours   MILES/TIME

THUR.

COURSE/NOTES _____

Visited Dr House he suspects low grade bronchitis
On waking no energy, slightly achy very tired
Coughing tight chest
7°C @ 1525 (B) Overcast   slept 8 hours   MILES/TIME

DATE _Jan 10 97_   **F**RI.

COURSE/NOTES _____

Headache most of the evening
     Raining   Slept 6hours   MILES/TIME

DATE _Jan. 11 97_   **S**AT.

COURSE/NOTES _____

3°C @ 0848 (B) Overcast   Slept 9½ hours   MILES/TIME

DATE _Jan. 12 97_   **S**UN.

COURSE/NOTES _____

10°C @ 1622 (B) Sunny   Slept 8hour   MILES/TIME

REVIEW

GOALS/NOTES _____

WEIGHT   CUMULATIVE TOTAL   WEEKLY TOTAL

cycle 21H

MON.

COURSE/NOTES _____

-20C @ 0638 (B) Mostly clear slept 6½ hours
MILES/TIME

TUES.

COURSE/NOTES _____

-20C @ 0826 (B)   Sunny   Slept 7 hours
MILES/TIME

WED.

COURSE/NOTES _____

Feeling worse than last 2 days!
Feel very tired no energy
-30C @ 0748 (B) clear-sunny   slept 7½ hours
MILES/TIME

THUR.

COURSE/NOTES Worked out in evening
20:46 on step machine
Lower back feels sore

-30C @ 0811 (B) Partly cloudy slept 7½ hours
MILES/TIME

DATE Jan. 17, 1997   **F**RI.

COURSE/NOTES _____
_____
_____
_____
Lower back sore
Feel tired
Soc @ 0715 (B)   Raining   Slept 8 hours
                                          MILES/TIME [   ]

DATE Jan. 18 97   **S**AT.

COURSE/NOTES _____
_____
_____
No head cold symptoms
Feel a little less tired
4°C @ 0950 (B) Raining   Slept 9 hours
                                          MILES/TIME [   ]

DATE Jan. 19 97   **S**UN.

COURSE/NOTES Worked out in evening
  27.49.99 on step machine
_____
No head cold symptoms yesterday
Not much coughing yesterday
No head cold symptoms this morning
Feel a little better still not 100%
7.5°C @ 0946 (B) Raining   Slept 8 hours
                                          MILES/TIME [   ]

                                                          REVIEW

GOALS/NOTES _____
_____
_____
_____
_____
_____

WEIGHT [   ]   CUMULATIVE
                    TOTAL [   ]   WEEKLY
                                       TOTAL [   ]

                    Cycle 214

MON.

COURSE/NOTES _____

5°c @ 0716 (?)   Overcast   Slept 7 hours   MILES/TIME

TUES.

DATE Jan. 21, 87

COURSE/NOTES Ran with Graeme for 1:05.09
Ran slow 9-10 minute mile pace. Felt very good
Estimated distance 11-12K

Asics 123 ~~50~~

4°c @ 0528   Raining   Slept 5½ hours   MILES/TIME   11.5K

WED.

DATE Jan. 22, 97

COURSE/NOTES Around Elm Park
Walk 7.15.55   Lap 1 3.13.42,   Lap 2 3.02.22,   Lap 3 3.02.5
Lap 4 3.04.38,   Lap 5 3.08.98, Lap 6 3.04.36,
Lap 7 2.57.47   Walk 2 5.00.00
Total Run 3½ M   21,33.36

- Sore lower back after run   Asics 125 4.5K
30°c @ 0647 (?) Overcast   Slept 6½ hours   MILES/TIME   4K

THUR.

DATE Jan. 23, 1987

COURSE/NOTES Forerunners Running Clinic
Pyramid/s x10 w/route warm up   400 metres,   600,   800,   1000,
800, 600, 400.   Last 400 @ 6:00 min/mile pace
Felt tired @ 0900. Lower back felt funny before running
the pyramid section - during warm up.

                        Partly cloudy   Jazz 53.45K
0°c @ 0601 (?) Mostly clear   Slept 7 hours   MILES/TIME   7.1K

DATE Jan. 24, 97   **F**RI.

COURSE/NOTES _____

Felt tired - from training session?
-20C @ 0744 Sunny   Slept 8 hours MILES/TIME

DATE Jan 25 97   **S**AT.

COURSE/NOTES _____

Quad's still sore
-70c @ 0844 Sunny   Slept 8 hours MILES/TIME

DATE Jan. 26, 97   **S**UN.

COURSE/NOTES _____

70C at end of run at home Sunny   Asics 125 21.5
-11°C on radio downtown
-90c @ 0745 Clear-Sunny Slept 7½ hours MILES/TIME   17k 1:32.2?

REVIEW

GOALS/NOTES _____

WEIGHT ____   CUMULATIVE TOTAL 39.6h   WEEKLY TOTAL 39.6h

Cycle 21h

MON.

COURSE/NOTES _____

-5.5°C@ 0740 Overcast slept 6 hours   MILES/TIME

TUES.

COURSE/NOTES _____

Tired
sore (slightly) lower back
3°@ 0810 (B) Overcast   slept 7 hours   MILES/TIME

WED.

COURSE/NOTES _____

Feel fine
slightly sore lower back
4.5°C @ 0735 (B)   Overcast   slept 7 hours   MILES/TIME

THUR.

COURSE/NOTES _____

Feel tired
6°C @ 0641 (B) overcast slept 7½ hours   MILES/TIME

DATE _Jan-31_ **FRI.**

COURSE/NOTES _Richmond Kajaks Ice Breaker 10k_
course 58.06.41

Sore right hip during run
Sore right knee after run
3°C @ 0531 Cloudy   Slept 5½ hours   MILES/TIME

Shadow II 10k
10k
58.06.41

DATE _Feb.1_ **SAT.**

Ran ≈ 4.5k   walked ≈ 2k
COURSE/NOTES walk 7.27.92 , ½k 3.06.33 , ½k 3.14.87 , ½k 3.22.2,
½k 3.20.08 ,   3.36.37 , w ½k 7.05.78

Sore lower back
Sore left foot
4.5°C @ 0813 (B)   Overcast Slept 8 hours   MILES/TIME

Asics 125 28k
4.5k run
6.5k total

DATE _Feb.2_ **SUN.**

COURSE/NOTES Kajaks Ice-Breaker 10k race
≈ 45.50   1k 4.08   1 mile 6.56, 2k 8.56.40 2nd k 4.48
3k 13.26.74 3rd k 4.30.34, 4k 17.55.61 4.28.87, 5k 22.36.66
4.41.05, 6k 27.45.50, 5.08.87, 7k 32.15.18, 4.29.66 8k 36.48.04
4.32.85, 41.22.46 4.34.41, 9k 41.22.45 ≈ 4.25 10k ≈ 45.50
Personal course record

2°C @ 0710 (B) Clear   Slept 6½ hours   MILES/TIME

Jazz (2/4) 5.45 k
10k

REVIEW

GOALS/NOTES

WEIGHT

CUMULATIVE TOTAL 6 8.1k

WEEKLY TOTAL 28.5k

cycle 21k

MON.

COURSE/NOTES _____

-10°C @ 0650 (B) clear   slept 7 hours   MILES/TIME

TUES.

DATE Feb. 4

COURSE/NOTES Graeme's Health Club around sea wall, counter clockwise
to Park Headquarters back to Graeme's Health Club
walk 3.57, Slow run to mile 0 4.06 0.8 km marker 45.15.41
Total to 8km marker 53.19.08, Back to mile 0 1:04.45, End 1:12.27
walk 5.50

ASICS 125   40

-4°C @ 0523 (B) clear   slept 6½ hours   MILES/TIME   12.25K

WED.

DATE Feb. 5

COURSE/NOTES Around Neighbourhood
Total time 39.58.95 3. Walk 5.33.60 2.Run 28.10.86
1. walk 6.14.55
Total Walk ~~~~ 11.48.15

Shadow II
Saucony Grid 15.5

-4°C @ 0524 (B) clear   slept 6 hours   MILES/TIME   5.5K

THUR.

DATE Feb. 6

COURSE/NOTES Interval workout run 40 seconds walk
10 seconds slow jog 10 seconds x 15 times

Jazz 70.45

-4 @ 0723 (B) sunny   slept 5½ hours   MILES/TIME   5K

DATE _Feb. 7_ **F**RI.

COURSE/NOTES _____
_____
_____
_____
_____
_____
1°C @ 0700 (0) Mixed rain & snow Slept 6¼ hours ___ MILES/TIME

DATE _Feb. 8_ **S**AT.

COURSE/NOTES _____
_____
_____
_____
_____
0°C @ 0824 (B) Overcast Slept 6½ hours ___ MILES/TIME

DATE _Feb. 9_ **S**UN.

COURSE/NOTES Ran with Baby Jogger for first time
Walk 5/0.24 Run 43.48.²³, Walk 6.13.24
Shaughnessy 5K 27.26.28
_____
_____
                                          NB825 7.2K
-10°C @ 0852 (B)   Slept 7½ hours   7.2K 55.11.71
                          MILES/TIME

REVIEW

GOALS/NOTES _____
_____
_____
_____
_____
_____

WEIGHT [   ]   CUMULATIVE TOTAL 98.05K   WEEKLY TOTAL 29.95K
                                                          58.1
                  Cycle 21K

MON.

DATE Feb. 10

COURSE/NOTES

Felt sick - Flu like symptoms at dinner time
felt weak no energy and achy muscles

-0.5°C @ 0626 (B) Partly Cloudy 5½ cloud/½ clear Slept 6½ hours

MILES/TIME

TUES.

DATE Feb. 11

COURSE/NOTES

Felt weak and achy also my throat feels off
1°C @ 0825 (B) Raining Slept 10 hours

MILES/TIME

WED.

DATE Feb. 12

COURSE/NOTES

Felt better (some) what in the evening between 6-10

3°C @ 1007 (B) Sunny Slept 6½ hours

MILES/TIME

THUR.

DATE Feb. 13

COURSE/NOTES

Felt worse, the last evening achy plus cough and
head cold symptoms runny nose sputum but not very
green

20°C @ 0919 (B) Raining slept 8 hours

MILES/TIME

DATE Feb.14 **F**RI.

COURSE/NOTES _____

2°C @ 0837 (B) Raining   Slept 8 hours   MILES/TIME

DATE Feb.15 **S**AT.

COURSE/NOTES _____

7°C @ 1048 (B) Mostly Cloudy   High Cloud   Slept 9 hours   MILES/TIME

DATE Feb.16 **S**UN.

COURSE/NOTES _____

4°C @ 0923 (B) Overcast   Slept 9 hours   MILES/TIME

REVIEW

GOALS/NOTES _____

WEIGHT _____   CUMULATIVE TOTAL 98.05   WEEKLY TOTAL _____

Cycle 2/1

Above: Yobes Ondeiki at the 1993 Gasparilla 15km road race, Tampa, Florida. Right: Suzy Favor-Hamilton leads Alisa Hill in the 1992 Olympic Trials 1500 meters, New Orleans, Louisiana.

"The race may not be to the swift nor the victory to the strong, but that's how you bet."

-Damon Runyon

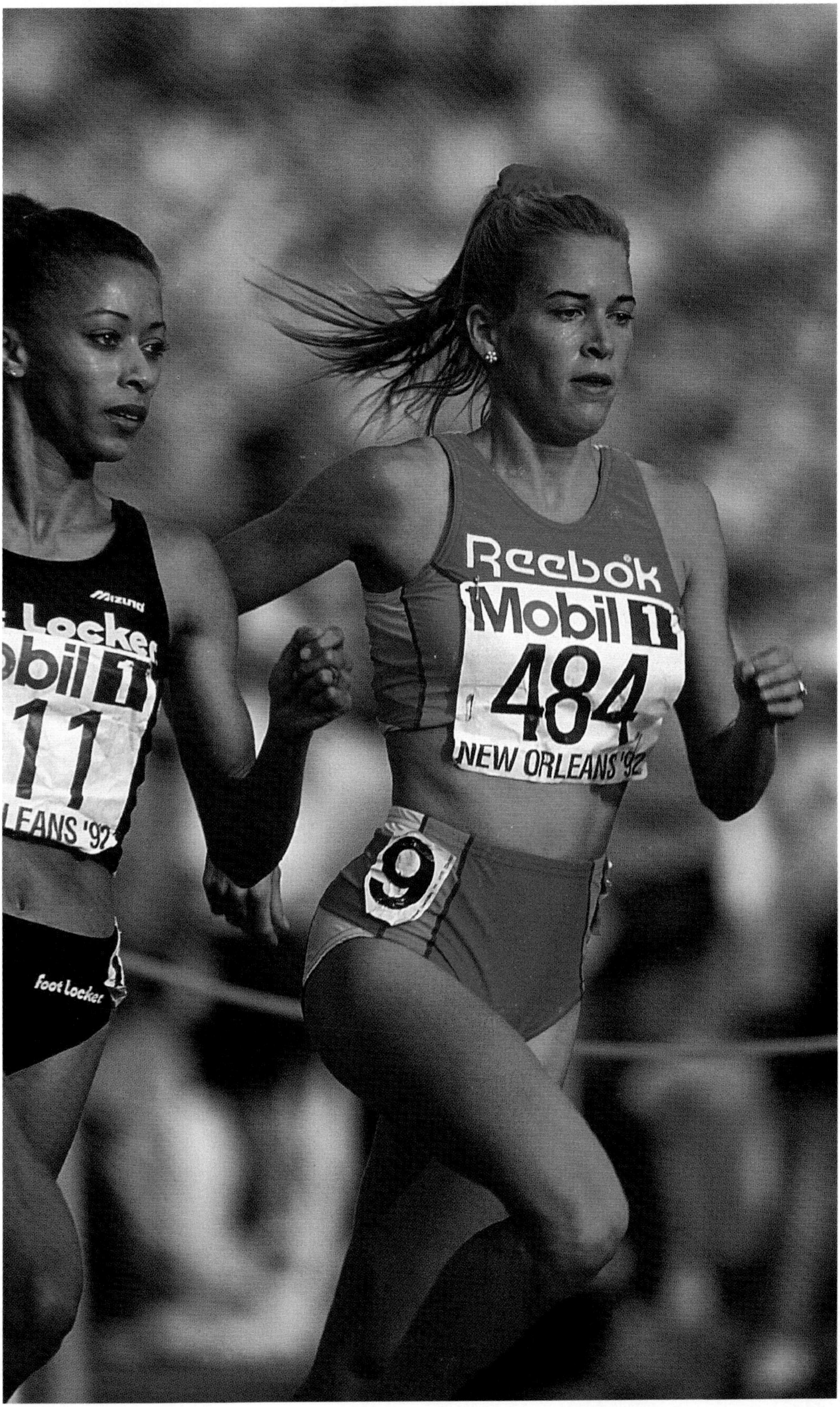
Reebok
Mobil 1
484
NEW ORLEANS '92
9
foot Locker

Argentina harrier goes over the barrier in the junior men's 1993 World Cross Country Championships, Amorebieta, Spain.

"No one knows what he can do until he tries."

-Latin proverb

MON.

DATE Feb. 17

COURSE/NOTES

Still feel sick. Feel worse than Sat and Sun

4°C @ 0836 (B) Sunny/cloudy slept 8 hours   MILES/TIME

TUES.

DATE Feb. 18

COURSE/NOTES

3°C @ 0849 (B) Overcast slept 5½ hours   MILES/TIME

WED.

DATE Feb. 19

COURSE/NOTES

Felt very spaced out upon waking

Overcast   slept 8 hours   MILES/TIME

THUR.

DATE Feb. 20

COURSE/NOTES

Felt very spaced out upon waking but not quite
as yesterday

0°C @ 082? (B) Sunny   slept 8 hours   MILES/TIME

DATE ___Feb. 21___   **F**RI.

COURSE/NOTES _____
_____
_____
_____

Feel better_____
20C @ 0833 (B) Overcast Slept 7½ hours
                                        MILES/TIME

DATE ___Feb. 22___   **S**AT.

COURSE/NOTES _____
Feel sick again head cold symptoms runny nose,
cough, coughing up sputum
Shawn has a cold
Katelyn has a cold
10C @ 0915 (B) Sunny   Slept 6 hours
                                        MILES/TIME

DATE ___Feb. 23___   **S**UN.

COURSE/NOTES _____
Still have a cold runny nose slight cough, coughing
up sputum
Katelyn has a cold
Shawn has a cold

10C @ 0852 (B) Sunny   Slept 7 hours
                                        MILES/TIME

                                                      REVIEW

GOALS/NOTES _____
_____
_____
_____
_____

WEIGHT [   ]   CUMULATIVE   98 05   WEEKLY
                      TOTAL   98.05   TOTAL
                              cycle 21k

MON.

DATE Feb 24

COURSE/NOTES Head cold symptoms

-2°C @ 0617 (B) clear Slept 7 3/4 hours   MILES/TIME

TUES.

DATE Feb 25

COURSE/NOTES Head cold symptoms

-0.5°C @ 0628 (B) clear Slept 6 1/2 hours   MILES/TIME

WED.

DATE Feb 26

COURSE/NOTES Still have head cold symptoms sore throat, loss of voice

Ran new course to 33rd Ave   Walk 6.23.14, Run 26.26.71,
Walk 2.00.88, Run 10.58.46, Walk 2.60.65, Run 17.56.84,
Walk 2.44.00,
0°C @ 0748 (B) Sunny   Slept 8 hours   MILES/TIME 10K 1:08.

Shadow II 25.5

THUR.

DATE Feb 27

COURSE/NOTES Ran walked 1:14
Interval work out   4 x 400 run 70% walk 400m
300m @ 75% walk 300m, 200 m @ 80% walk 200m
100m @ 90% walk 100m

-1.5°C @ 0633 (B) Mostly clear Slept 9 hours   MILES/TIME

NB 825 10K
10K
→ NB 825 17.2K
Total

DATE __Feb 28__ **F**RI.

COURSE/NOTES _____
_____
_____
_____
_____

-2°C @ 0627 (B) Overcast   slept 6½ hours MILES/TIME

__March 1__
DATE ~~Feb~~ **S**AT.

COURSE/NOTES _____
_____
_____
_____
_____

-3°@ 0700 (B) Raining   slept 7¼ hours MILES/TIME

DATE __March 2__ **S**UN.

COURSE/NOTES Centipedes Sprint Classic 5k
Official time 21.23 my watch 1 mile 6.31.97
5k 21.30.81
_____
_____

                                    Asics Gel Racer 8
                                    racer
10c @ 0701 (B) Raining   slept 7¼ hours   10k
                                   MILES/TIME
                                    Asics 123 505k

REVIEW

GOALS/NOTES _____
_____
_____
_____
_____

WEIGHT [ ]   CUMULATIVE TOTAL 128.05   WEEKLY TOTAL 30k
                cycle 21k   98.05
                                                   128.05

MON.

COURSE/NOTES

Left lower leg muscle above ankle slightly
behind ankle but not achilles tendon sore

-10°C @ 0618 B   Overcast   Slept 6½ hours
MILES/TIME

TUES.

COURSE/NOTES Ran slowly with Graeme. Graeme felt
bad - Stomach cramps. Ran from Graeme's Health
Club to Eastern half of Stanley park slowed back Pipeline
Lower leg muscle
Lower leg muscle felt good during run
Same muscle as above still sore before run   Asics 125 47

-5°C @ 0546   Clear   Slept 6¾   MILES/TIME   1h 48.28.75

WED.

COURSE/NOTES

-10°C @ 0633 (B)   Overcast   Slept 6¾
MILES/TIME

THUR.

COURSE/NOTES Running class 10 min warm up
20 hilling terrain, 10 minutes cool down

Left foot center bottom upon arising   Size 97.45

2°C @ 0712 (B)   Raining   Slept 8½   MILES/TIME   7k

DATE March 7   **F**RI.

COURSE/NOTES _____

0°C @ 0630   Overcast   slept 7 hrs   MILES/TIME | |

DATE March 8   **S**AT.

COURSE/NOTES Walk ~45 minutes around Stanley Park
Run 44.03.84 minutes through Stanley Park Trails very
fast pace with Graeme.
Feel like I might be getting sick again, thick saliva
coming from throat, very tired, run down feeling
Muscles sore from 2nd workout above

3° @ 0656 (R)   Partly cloudy   slept 6 hrs   MILES/TIME | 25 58.25 R | 11k |

DATE March 9 97   **S**UN.

COURSE/NOTES Still feel tired, muscles in hips & buttocks
feel slightly sore

2° @ 0701 (B)   Overcast   slept 8 hrs   MILES/TIME | |

REVIEW

GOALS/NOTES _____

| WEIGHT | | CUMULATIVE TOTAL | 193.05 | WEEKLY TOTAL | 25k |

cycle 21k   118.05

MON.

COURSE/NOTES

-2°C @ 0656 (B) Turned into a sunny day
Overcast   slept 6 1/2 hours MILES/TIME

TUES.

COURSE/NOTES

Feel tired

-1°C @ 0600 Overcast   slept 7 1/2 hours MILES/TIME

Jazz 88.2
10.75 / 1:01.23

WED.

COURSE/NOTES

Feel tired - Feel like I'm not getting enough sleep

-2.5°C @ 0618 Overcast   slept 6 1/2 hours MILES/TIME

THUR.

COURSE/NOTES Fartlek workout warm up for 10 min
Run for 20 min cool down for walk
Head cold symptoms nose congested throat has sputum.

-3°C @ 0654 Raining slept 8 hours MILES/TIME

NB 825 23K
5K 43 min

DATE _March 14_ **F**RI.

COURSE/NOTES _____

congested nose sputum in throat

@ 0630

−5.50 (B) clear   Slept 6 hours   MILES/TIME

DATE _March 15_ **S**AT.

COURSE/NOTES _____

@ 0703

−2.50 (B) Snowing •   Slept 6¾ hour MILES/TIME

DATE _March 16_ **S**UN.

COURSE/NOTES _____

still have head cold symptoms

Thin crust of snow on ground

−10C @ 0855 (B) Sunny Slept 7 hours MILES/TIME

REVIEW

GOALS/NOTES _____

WEIGHT [   ]   CUMULATIVE TOTAL 168.8   WEEKLY TOTAL 15.75

153.05
168.8

MON.

COURSE/NOTES

0°C @ 0658 (B)   Raining   slept 6½ hours
MILES/TIME

TUES.

COURSE/NOTES

3.5°C @ 0643 (B)   Raining heavily   slept 7½ hours
MILES/TIME

WED.

COURSE/NOTES New Course Walk 5.00.41 Ran 1:00.99
31.14.30 to 41st Ave   44.15.79 to St Georges
51.22.92 to Dunbar + 31st Ave

shadow 717.1

6°C @ 0649 (B)   Raining   slept 7½ hours
MILES/TIME 11.5M 1:06.40

THUR.

COURSE/NOTES Pyramid 400m, 800m, 1600m, 800m, 400m
333.32   7:10   334.60   1.41.0

Felt stiff from yesterdays run all over
1.5°C @ 0718 (B)   Mostly Cloudy   slept 7½ hours
MILES/TIME

NB 825 28k

5k

DATE March 21   **FR**I.

COURSE/NOTES _____

2.5°C @ 0911   Overcast   Slept 7 hours   MILES/TIME

DATE March 22   **S**AT.

COURSE/NOTES 1km to 6km warm of Sun Run Run
5k 25.
Sore left leg on inside of main bone about
half way between ankle and knee. Shin splints?
Feels like a muscle rather than the bone
            125   65.25

-1°C @ 0721 (B)   Overcast   slept 7½ hours   MILES/TIME   7h 40.33.36

DATE March 23   **S**UN.

COURSE/NOTES 10k 45.05.06 on watch packed watch late
1st mile 6.59.21, 5k 21.52.05, 1 mile left 37.52.38
last mile 7.12.68]
False Creek 10k
Hamstring on right leg sore
                                NB825 39k

-10°C @ 0619 (B)   clear   slept 6½ hours   MILES/TIME   11k

REVIEW

GOALS/NOTES _____

WEIGHT   CUMULATIVE TOTAL 203.3   WEEKLY TOTAL 34.5
                                                 168.8
                                                 203.3

MON.

DATE March 24

COURSE/NOTES _____

_____

_____

_____

_____

0°C @ 0629 (B) Overcast slept 6½ hours | MILES/TIME |

TUES.

DATE March 25

COURSE/NOTES Ran with Graeme from his health club
through trail up to Prospect Point down to 2nd
to sea wall at 4th beach back around sea wall to
Graeme's health club

_____

3°C @ 0557 (B) overcast slept 6¾ hours | MILES/TIME | Jazz 99.45 / 11:25 1:05.14 K |

WED.

DATE March 26

COURSE/NOTES _____

_____

_____

_____

5°C (am radio)
7°C @ 0713 (B) overcast slept 6½ hours | MILES/TIME |

THUR.

DATE March 27

COURSE/NOTES 5K 43:23 actual time predicted time
45:45

Sore butt right hand side.

_____

Overcast   slept 7 hours | MILES/TIME | 123 500h / 5K 43:23 / 6K |

DATE March 28   **F**RI.

COURSE/NOTES   Measured new running route at 11.5k
rode course twice second time 11.5k in 41.0 minutes

Legs not sore on 8kips
Felt good after ride

Partly Cloudy
5°C @ 0754 (B) + TV   Sunny   Slept 7 hours   MILES/TIME

23K cycling

DATE March 29   **S**AT.

COURSE/NOTES   3h 14.52.18   3to4h 4.46.08   4h 19.38.26
4to5h 4.33.33   5h 24.11.59.   5to6h 4.58.58   6h 29.10.17
6to7h 4.49.25   7h 33.59.42   7to8h 4.39.34   8h 38.38.76
8to9h 4.51.71   9h 43.30.47   9to10h 4.43.54
10h 48.14.01

Sore left leg - shin between ankle and knee
Sore butt both sides especially right side
0.5°C @ 0722 (B)   overcast   Slept 7½ hours   MILES/TIME

10k ▮▮▮
48.14.01

DATE March 30   **S**UN.

COURSE/NOTES

3.5°C @ 0858 (B)   Sunny/ Partly Cloudy   Slept 7½ hours   MILES/TIME

REVIEW

GOALS/NOTES

WEIGHT   CUMULATIVE TOTAL   230.55   WEEKLY TOTAL   27.25
203.3

cycle 44k

MON. * wore shorts for 1st time

DATE March 31

COURSE/NOTES Ran with Graeme from Aquatic center east around
False Creek west to Vanier Park Kits beach Jericho beach
and stopped at Jericho beach due to blister. Blister caused
by new shoe fitting snug? Used Thorlo socks

* Blister on right foot on bottom of foot at junction of 1st (big) & 2nd toe
30 on TV   wore shorts for first time   Shadow II 36.5ki
-6° wind chill on TV   Sunny in late morning
-2°C @ 0615 (B) Overcast/raining Slept 6¼ hours MILES/TIME 1:08. 11k

TUES.

DATE April 1

COURSE/NOTES

Used doughnut shaped corn pad on foot where blister is
located; which worked very well
Chafing on inside of both thighs
Sore 2nd toe on left foot
Feel tired due to Shaun waking me up 3 to 4 times
1.5°C @ 0722 (B) Sunny   Slept 5½ hours MILES/TIME

WED.

DATE April 2

COURSE/NOTES

Felt tired. Got up at 0200 walked around with Shaun with
lullaby music and gave him the cold plastic waxleaf book
Shaun's teething!
-2°C @ 0658 (B) Overcast Slept 6½ hours MILES/TIME

THUR.

DATE April 3

COURSE/NOTES

-10°C @ 0538 (B)   Partly cloudy Slept 6¾ hours MILES/TIME

DATE Apri| 4 **F**RI.

COURSE/NOTES _____
_____
_____
_____

1° C @ 0614 CBC
-5°C @ 0614 (B)   Sunny   Slept 6½ hours MILES/TIME

DATE Apri| 5 **S**AT.

COURSE/NOTES North Shore 5K watch 20:01.92 punched
watch 1-2 seconds late
R Official time 19:58 !!

NB825 41.5K
1°C Downtown 20°C Airport Chwx @ 0608   5K + 25k
-4.5°C @ 0608 (B)   Sunny   Slept 6½ hours MILES/TIME   ASICS Gel Raco 9

DATE Apri| 6 **S**UN.
Daylight Savings Time begins

COURSE/NOTES _____
_____
_____
_____

5°C @ 0755 (B)   Sunny   Slept 6½ hours MILES/TIME

REVIEW

GOALS/NOTES _____
_____
_____
_____
_____

WEIGHT | CUMULATIVE TOTAL 249.05 | WEEKLY TOTAL 18.5h
cycle 44h | 230.55h

*Above: Meghan Flowers on the third leg of the winning 4 x 1,500 meter
women's relay team, 1993 Penn Relays, Philadelpia, Pennsylvania.
Right: Todd Williams in the 1993 World Cross Country Championships,
Amorebieta, Spain.*

"The secret of staying young is to live
honestly, eat slowly and
lie about your age."

-Lucille Ball

Competitor in the 1992 Bobby Crim 10 mile road race, Flint, Michigan.

"Old age is the only disease you don't look forward to being cured of."

-From the movie Citizen Kane.

MON.

Fraser River - Pacific Spirit course

DATE April 7

COURSE/NOTES Walk 5.30.33, 41st Ave 32.00.52
Clinton sign post 36.45.27; St Georges school 44.04.60
Dunbar st. 50.42.63. Finish 1:04.29

-4°C @ 0618 CBC Radio
-2.5°@ 0624 B clear   Slept 7 hours

	Jazz	110.95
MILES/TIME	11.5k	1:04.29

TUES.

DATE April 8

COURSE/NOTES Ran with Graeme - the usual health club
route around the seawall counter clockwise

8°C @ 0600 weather channel
10°C @ 0559 (B) overcast   Slept 4½ hours

	25	77.0
MILES/TIME	11.75k	58.00.3

WED.

DATE April 9

COURSE/NOTES

0°C @ 0708 Overcast   Slept 9 hours

MILES/TIME		

THUR.

DATE April 10

COURSE/NOTES Ran Park trails with Graeme

7°C @ 0600 on weather channel
-1.5°@ 0559 (B) Partly cloudy Slept

	Jazz	121.45
MILES/TIME	10.5k	54.12.90

DATE _April 11_ **F**RI.

COURSE/NOTES _Kelowna_
_____
_____
_____
_____
_____ MILES/TIME [ ]

DATE _April 12_ **S**AT.

COURSE/NOTES _Kelowna   skiing at Big White_
_____
_____
_____
_____
_____ MILES/TIME [ ]

DATE _April 13_ **S**UN.

COURSE/NOTES _____
_____
_____
_____
_____
_____ MILES/TIME [ ]

REVIEW

GOALS/NOTES _____
_____
_____
_____
_____

WEIGHT [ ]   CUMULATIVE TOTAL [278.8]   WEEKLY TOTAL [29.75]
Cycle 44k   249.05
                                                      278.8

MON.

DATE April/14

COURSE/NOTES Sun Fun Run Course warm up 6.

Lap 1k 4. 2k 4, 3k 457.77 205f.81 4k 504.73

5k 4.57.99, 6k 5.30.13, 7k 5.06.84, 8k 4.50.56,

9k 5.14.49 10k 4.29.84

7°C @ 0600 Radio & TV Overcast slept 6 hours

125.88h
10k 49.
11k total

MILES/TIME

TUES.

DATE April 15

COURSE/NOTES Feel tired

8°C @ 0600 TV Raining slept 7½ hours

MILES/TIME

WED.

DATE April 16

COURSE/NOTES

12°C @ 0816 CBC Airport Overcast slept 3½ hours

MILES/TIME

THUR.

DATE April 17

COURSE/NOTES

7°C @ 0706 TV A few clouds Mostly clear slept 8½ hours

MILES/TIME

DATE April 18   **F**RI.

COURSE/NOTES _walk with baby jogger 5.10.43_
Run 24:00 min walk 25:00 min Run 5:00.72
Run 1/2h 2.54.09 walk 5:30.00

125 90.5K

0°C @   Sunny   slept 3 1/2 hours   MILES/TIME   2.5h

DATE April 19   **S**AT.

COURSE/NOTES _____

6°C @ 0645 TV Overcast slept 6 1/2 hour   MILES/TIME

DATE April 20   4.13.²   **SUN.**

COURSE/NOTES 1K 3.45? 2K 7.58.51 3K 2.12
4K 16.54.67 5K 04.10 20.58.79 6K 4.41.68 25.40.48
7K 4.06.61 29.47.09 8K 4.12.93 34.00.02 9K 4.18.31
38.19.33 10K 3.52.27 42.11.60   42.05 official time
1 mile 6.11   4.12/km   6.48/mile   Asics Gel

Sore right knee after race   12h total
6°C @ 0510   slept   MILES/TIME 10K 42.11.60

                                                Racer 10

                                                          REVIEW

GOALS/NOTES _____

WEIGHT   CUMULATIVE TOTAL   304.3   WEEKLY TOTAL   25.5 K
                                                                278.8
                                                                304.3

MON.

COURSE/NOTES

Quads sore in afternoon
Feel tired
Sore bottom of right foot!

3° downtown radio
5°C @ 0541 Partly cloudy Slept 6½ hours MILES/TIME
Airport Radio

TUES.

DATE April 22

COURSE/NOTES Sore bottom of right foot upon rising
Foot was not sore after riding bike

6°C @ 0600 Sunny Slept 6½ hour MILES/TIME Bike 230k

WED.

DATE April 23

COURSE/NOTES Sore bottom of right foot

8°C @ 0711 cnwx Sunny Slept 6½ hours MILES/TIME

THUR.

DATE April 24

COURSE/NOTES Sore bottom of right foot not as
sore as yesterday

Overcast Slept 5 hour MILES/TIME

DATE April 25 **F**RI.

COURSE/NOTES _____

10°C @ 0615 Raining lightly Slept 8½ hour MILES/TIME | bike 76.4k |

DATE April 26 **S**AT.

COURSE/NOTES _____

12°C @ 0900 Overcast Slept 8½ hour MILES/TIME

DATE April 27 **S**UN.

COURSE/NOTES Shawn woke me up @ 0300 I went back
to sleep @ 0500

°C @ sunny slept MILES/TIME

REVIEW

GOALS/NOTES _____

WEIGHT | | CUMULATIVE TOTAL | 304.3k | WEEKLY TOTAL | ~~304.3k~~ |
cycle 90.4k

304.3k
cycle 46.4k

MON.

DATE April 28

COURSE/NOTES _Susan woke me up @ ~ 0300_

Radio
8°C @ 0752 Raining   Slept 6 hour   MILES/TIME

TUES.

DATE April 29

COURSE/NOTES _Ran with Graeme from his health club_
around the seawall counterclockwise and back to
his health club. Ran slowly felt great.
Right knee twinging after the run while driving
home
6.50.97 to mile 0!   Stanley Pk 48.25
6°C @ 0643 Partly Cloudy slept 5½ hour   1:08.52
                                  MILES/TIME   11.75 m

WED.

DATE April 30

COURSE/NOTES

Airport Chux
7°C @ 0606   Overcast   Slept 7 hour   MILES/TIME

THUR.

DATE May 1

COURSE/NOTES _Ran Pacific Spirit Race route_

Airport 6hux   Jazz 132.45
8°C @ 0551   Overcast   slept 6 hour   10k 56.01.31
6°C Downtown   MILES/TIME

DATE __May 2__ **F**RI.

COURSE/NOTES __Seattle__
_____
_____
_____
_____
_____
Slept 6 hour __MILES/TIME__ [   ]

DATE __May 3__ **S**AT.

COURSE/NOTES __Seattle__
_____
_____
_____
_____
_____
Slept 6 hour MILES/TIME [   ]

DATE __May 4__ **S**UN.

COURSE/NOTES Shaughnessy 5K course plus down Vine St
to Maple Grove Park around park back to Bagel
Garden 1 mile 9.4584, 2h 11.58.12, 3h 17.35.33,
4h 23.16.30, 5h 28.55.18 ~10h 52.34.37

Weather Overcast | 25 - 100.5 k |
9°C @ 0800   Overcast   Slept 6½ hour MILES/TIME | 90h 52.3437 |

REVIEW

GOALS/NOTES _____
_____
_____
_____
_____
_____

WEIGHT [   ]   CUMULATIVE TOTAL [33 5.05h]   WEEKLY TOTAL [30.75h]
                            Cycle 90.4   304.3

MON.

DATE May 5

COURSE/NOTES

11°C @ 0713 CBC   Raining   Slept 7 hours   MILES/TIME

TUES.

DATE May 6

COURSE/NOTES Run with Graeme from bus health club
through park trails back to health club.
Right knee sore after running as usual!

10°C @ Airport
Downtown
7°C @ 0553   Overcast   Slept 5½ hours   MILES/TIME | Jazz 143.7 Km 58.41.55 11.25/1

WED.

DATE May 7

COURSE/NOTES Ran Pacific Spirit Race route

weather channel
8° @ 0620   Overcast   Slept 7 hours   MILES/TIME | Alfresco 10k 10k 49.57.11

THUR.

DATE May 8

COURSE/NOTES

7°C @ 0710 CBC   Sunny   Slept 6½ hours   MILES/TIME

DATE __May 9__   **F**RI.

COURSE/NOTES __Rode bike 17. km__

__Weather Channel__
__12°C @ 0612__   Mostly Cloudy Slept 6 hour   MILES/TIME

DATE __May 10__   **S**AT.

COURSE/NOTES __Pacific Spirit Race 10k__
Felt left hip and right knee after race, stretched
after race and these issues were resolved.
Went out too fast. 5h in 20.06.93 ! My 2nd fastest
5h time.   Felt left lower leg after warm up.
                                        Alfresco 23k
__Weather Channel__ Some high-thin clouds hours   10k
__10°C @ 0653__   Sunny Slept 7½   MILES/TIME   44.37.8

DATE __May 11__   **S**UN.

COURSE/NOTES _____

__11°C @ 0715__   Sunny   Slept 6½ hours   MILES/TIME

                                                  REVIEW

GOALS/NOTES _____

WEIGHT	CUMULATIVE TOTAL	366.3	WEEKLY TOTAL	31.25
		ccycle 107.4		335.05
				176

MON.

COURSE/NOTES Shaughessy 5K
Felt shin on left lower leg mid inside

13°C on CHWX
Weather Channel
11°C @ 0630   Sunny   Slept 7 hours   MILES/TIME

Shadow II 5545
1.2K 4.10.79
5K 24.23.00

TUES.

DATE May 13

COURSE/NOTES

Outside of left foot sore
Lower back sore

CHWX Downtown
14°C @ 0630   Sunny   Slept 7 hours   MILES/TIME

WED.

DATE May 14

COURSE/NOTES Ride Bike 18.1 km
Upon arising outside left foot sore
Lower back sore

CBC Airport
14°C @ 0607   Mostly Overcast Slept 7¼ hours   MILES/TIME

Ride 18.1 km

THUR.

DATE May 15

COURSE/NOTES Lower back not sore
Felt refreshed after 8 hours sleep

17°C @ 0813 Mostly Overcast Slept 8 hours   MILES/TIME

DATE _May 16_   **F**RI.

COURSE/NOTES _____

_____

_____

Outside right foot sore.

_____
                              Some high clouds
12°C @ 0600 Sunny   Slept 6¼ hours
                                            MILES/TIME [   ]

DATE _May 17_   **S**AT.

COURSE/NOTES _____

_____

_____

140 C @ Airport
Downtown CBWX
15°C @ 0902   Sunny   Slept 9 hours
                                            MILES/TIME [   ]

DATE _May 18_   **S**UN.

COURSE/NOTES _____

_____

_____

_____

17°C @ 0837   Sunny   Slept 4 hours
                                            MILES/TIME [   ]

                                                                    REVIEW

GOALS/NOTES _____

_____

_____

_____

WEIGHT [   ]   CUMULATIVE TOTAL [373.5]   WEEKLY TOTAL [7.2 t]

Cycle 18.1/h   cycle 125.5   3663

MON.

DATE May 19

COURSE/NOTES Shaughnessy 5h

Felt left shin during run
Tendon back of left not sore after run
Sore back of left knee tendon up arise

11°C @ 0642 Sunny Partly Cloudy Slept 6½ hours

MILES/TIME
Shadow H 61.65
~~6.2h~~
5K 24.24.48
Cycle 9.8k

TUES.

DATE May 20

COURSE/NOTES

Chwx
11°C @ 0730   Slept 8½ hours

MILES/TIME

WED.

DATE May 21

COURSE/NOTES Shaughnessy 5h   2K 4.23.69
1K 5.02.47   1M 2.45.84   7.48.01   2K 1.38.15 9.26.16,
3K 4.14.47, 13.40.63, 4K 4.33.27 18.13.90,
5K 4.26.05, 22.39.95 lll Run/walk 8.15.21

CBC Radio
11° @ 0615   Overcast   Slept 7¼ hours

MILES/TIME
Jazz 150.9
~~7.2K~~
5K 22.39.95

THUR.

DATE May 22

COURSE/NOTES

CBe
11°C @ 0814 Sunny but mostly Slept 7½ hours
            overcast

MILES/TIME

DATE _May 23_   **F**RI.

COURSE/NOTES _____

_____

_____

_____

crwx
11°C @ 0837   Overcast   Slept 7½ hours
138 lbs ?   MILES/TIME

DATE _May 24_   **S**AT.

COURSE/NOTES _____

_____

_____

_____

weather channel
13°C @ 0936   Overcast   Slept 6½ hours
140 lbs ?   MILES/TIME

DATE _May 25_   **S**UN.

COURSE/NOTES Shaugnessy 5K Race 20.03 official time
R 1K 4.21.09   1Mile 6.40.47, 2K 3.47.60 8.08.69,
   3K 3.52.25   12.00.94, 4K 4.09.03 16.09.97
   5K 3.52.66   20.02.63

                                             Asics GelRacer 11
weather channel   5.5
12°C @ 0631   Overcast   Slept 6 hours   5K 20.02.63
140 lbs ?   MILES/TIME

                                                               REVIEW

GOALS/NOTES _____

_____

_____

_____

_____

WEIGHT	140 lbs	CUMULATIVE TOTAL	392.4K	WEEKLY TOTAL	18.9
			Cycle 1350.1 K		373.5

Above: Peter Renner and Delmir Dos Santos are the early leaders in the 1993 Los Angeles Marathon, Los Angeles, California. Right: Olympic Development Team member in the 4 x 400 meter relay, 1993 Penn Relays.

"The Good Lord never gives you more than you can handle. Unless you die of something."

-Guindon cartoon caption

Competitor in the 1992 Bobby Crim 10 mile road race brings his work on the road with him.

"Heaven never helps men who will not act."

-Sophocles

MON.

COURSE/NOTES _____

_____

_____

120c Downtown
Chuck Airport
130c @ 0722   Overcast   Slept 8 hours   MILES/TIME
138/63 ?

TUES.

COURSE/NOTES Ran Stanley Park Trails with Graeme

_____

_____

10°c Downtown
Airport   Shadow II 72.9k
12°c @ 0536 Partly cloudy Slept 6 hours   11.25~52.00
143.5 lbs @ Graeme's health club   MILES/TIME

WED.

COURSE/NOTES _____

_____

_____

Weather Channel
15°c @ 0631 Partly cloudy Slept 5½ hours   MILES/TIME

THUR.

COURSE/NOTES walk approx 2 miles or 3 km - raining lightly
Slightly twisted my right ankle on a tree root at
W.37th, & Elm
Walked for 37:30.00 in the evening. Right outside
(top) ankle noticeably sore, but only slightly in evening
                                            Jazz 153.9
15°c @ 0700   Overcast   Slept 7 hours   3 k 30.45.0
                                            MILES/TIME

DATE __May 30__   **F**RI.

COURSE/NOTES __Felt tired - did not sleep enough__
__My right ankle~~████~~ feels sore.__

_____

_____

16° @ 0550 Overcast Slept 6 hours MILES/TIME [ ]

DATE __May 31__   **S**AT.

COURSE/NOTES __Rode bike with sticks for ≳30.00 min in AM__
__Rode bike with sticks for ≤ 1:00.00 in late afternoon__

_____

_____

16° C @ 707 Weather channel
14° C @ 0701 Raining Slept 7 hours MILES/TIME [ ]
      Clear

DATE __June 1__   **S**UN.

COURSE/NOTES _____

_____

_____

_____

14° C @ 1030 Overcast Slept 9½ hours MILES/TIME [ ]

                                              REVIEW

GOALS/NOTES _____

_____

_____

_____

WEIGHT [ ]   CUMULATIVE [406·65]   WEEKLY [14.25]
                TOTAL   TOTAL
                                                  382·4
                                          Cycle 135.1

MON.
DATE June 2

COURSE/NOTES Feel tired stayed up until 0200 with Susan
Ankle felt mostly better in the evening
streched and strenghtened ankle in morning and
evening. Iced ankle @ 1030

* 16 hours of daylight Sunrise 0511 Sunset 2111
Weather Channel
12°C @ 0720 Raining Slept 5½ hours   MILES/TIME

TUES.
DATE June 3

COURSE/NOTES Feel tired. Ankle (right) stills feels
off a bit.
Cycle 1:10.56   Run 33.53
        29k   5k

	Jazz 158.9
	Cycle 29k
	Run 5k

15°C @ 0554 Raining Slept 6 hours   MILES/TIME

WED.
DATE June 4

COURSE/NOTES Slight pain in centre right back under
right shoulder blade.

13°C @ 0710 Overcast   Slept 7¾ hours   MILES/TIME

THUR.
DATE June 5

COURSE/NOTES Middle right back very sore. Constant
pain Cannot breath deeply without great pain. Feels like
someone is sticking a knife in my back.
Went to Dr. Avelar - he determined that I have a rib
that has come out of place.

Weather Channel
12°C @ 0720 Overcast   Slept 7 hours   MILES/TIME

DATE June 6   **F**RI.

COURSE/NOTES Back still sore but not as much as Thurs
_____
_____
_____

Weather Channel
11°C @ 0710   Overcast Slept 8½ hours   MILES/TIME

DATE June 7   **S**AT.

COURSE/NOTES Back still sore!
_____
_____
_____

12°C @ Airport
14°C @ 0822 Sunny / Partly Cloudy Slept 7 hours   MILES/TIME
Downtown

DATE June 8   **S**UN.

COURSE/NOTES Back still sore! Back felt better after Duathlon!
Locarno Beach Spring Duathlon 1:27.51 on my watch
  1:28 according to the announcer
1st 5k run 23:47, Bike/8k 41.35, 2nd 5k run 23:28

Weather Channel   NB 825 5.1k
12°C @ 0455 Partly Cloudy Slept 5 hours MILES/TIME 5k+5k
                                                     7.0k

                                                     REVIEW

GOALS/NOTES _____
_____
_____
_____
_____

WEIGHT [   ]   CUMULATIVE   421.65   WEEKLY   15k
                TOTAL   TOTAL
                    cycle 85.1   406.65
                                            cycle 135.1

MON.

COURSE/NOTES

Weather Channel
10°C @ 0620   Sunny   Slept 6½ hours   MILES/TIME

TUES.

DATE June 10

COURSE/NOTES Ran ~10k of Stanley Park trails with
Graeme.
Back slightly sore before run less so after run

Downtown CKWX
10°C @ 0541   Sunny   Slept 7 hours   MILES/TIME   Shadow II 83K
160c @ 0812 CBC   10k 51.14.03

WED.

DATE June 11

COURSE/NOTES

CBC radio
140C @ 0712   Sunny / Cloudy   Slept 7½ hours   MILES/TIME

THUR.

DATE June 12

COURSE/NOTES Forerunners ~~ Pyramid workout 200, 400,
600, 800, 800, 600, 400, 200 metres
Felt great, breathing was slow and steady. I felt
like my breathing just clicked in. Breathing out hard
breathing in deep.

CKWX Airport
13°C @ 0651   Over-cast   Slept 7 hours   MILES/TIME   NB825 59K
120 C @ 0642 Downtown   7K

DATE June 13   **FRI.**

COURSE/NOTES Felt tired in the morning upon waking. Felt like I
had slept deep and well.

140C@ 0712 Overcast Slept 7½ hours MILES/TIME
Sunrise 0507 Sunset 2119 Sunlight 16:12

DATE June 14   **S**AT.

COURSE/NOTES Great run Longest Day Course plus ½ of Plattle
spirit Course. Breathing great.
10K 48.36.58   5K ≈ 30.0   Total run with ≈ 1224

weather Channel   Shadows 98K
13°C @ 0650   Sunny   Slept 6 hour MILES/TIME ≈ 15K
Sunrise 0507 Sunset 2119 Sunlight 16:12

DATE June 15   **S**UN.

COURSE/NOTES Blister less sore. Sore muscle right lower
leg behind inside ankle achilles tendon or next to it

Airport chux
13°C @ 0730
16°C @ 0730   Sunny   Slept 7½ hours MILES/TIME
Downtown

                                                            REVIEW

GOALS/NOTES

WEIGHT	CUMULATIVE TOTAL	453.65	WEEKLY TOTAL	32 ft

421.65
cyc6 185.1

MON.

COURSE/NOTES Graeme's Heath club with Graeme around the
Seawall Counter Clockwise. Goal to run finishes at 7.52/mile
warmup 7.04.32, mile1 7.44.02, mile2 7.36.71, mile3 7.37.0,
mile4 7.45.77, mile5 7.45.42, cool down 16.54.09,

Downtown
14°C @ 0552
15°C @ 0532   Overcast   Slept 6 hours   MILES/TIME
Airport   Sunrise 0507 Sunset 2120 Sunshine 16:13

125	12.25
1:02.27
1.18h

TUES.

COURSE/NOTES Ran Longest Day route with Grant Wheeler
between 1800 and 1900

Weather Channel
16°C @ 0236   Overcast   Slept 8 hours   MILES/TIME
Sunrise 05:07 Sunset 2121   Sunshine 16:14

Jazz/68.4
57.02.98
OK

WED.

COURSE/NOTES

15°C @ 0716   Overcast   Slept 7 3/4 hours   MILES/TIME
Sunrise 0507 Sunset 2121   Sunshine 16:14

THUR.

COURSE/NOTES Did not sleep solid. Awoke many times
during the night

Weather Channel
13°C @ 0802 Overcast Slept 7 3/4 hours MILES/TIME
Sunrise 0507 Sunset 2121   Sunshine 16:14

DATE June 20   **FRI.**

COURSE/NOTES woke up at least twice at 0200 and 0400 to 0430
PR Official time 41.20 my watch 41.21.47 Longest Day 16h
Mile 1 6.28.69, Mile 2 6.23.10 12.51.79, Mile 3 7.16.29
20.08.08, 5k 20.48.74, Mile 4 7.14.99 27.23.07, Miles
6 35.26 33.58.33 Mile 5.2 1.20.45 35.18.78 Last Mile
6.02.69 !? 41.21.47   Asics Gel Race 12

12° @ 0800   Sunny/Partly Cloudy Slept 7½ hours   MILES/TIME   10k 4.2
Sunrise 0507 Sunset 2122 Sunshine 16:15   2k warmup

DATE June 21   **SAT.**

COURSE/NOTES Mountain biked with Bruce Law

Airport Crux
12°C @ 0751
10°C @ 0751   Overcast   Slept 7½ hours   MILES/TIME
Downtown   Cycle 22.25k 1:32.21

DATE June 22   **SUN.**

COURSE/NOTES Feel like I'm getting sick!

Weather Channel
14° @ 1052   Overcast
12°C @ 0615   Overcast   Slept 7½ hours   MILES/TIME
Sunset 0508   Sunset

REVIEW

GOALS/NOTES

WEIGHT   CUMULATIVE TOTAL 485.46 k   WEEKLY TOTAL 22.25 cycle / 31.75 run
                    207.35 k   Run 453.65k
                                      Bike 185.1

MON.

DATE June 23

COURSE/NOTES Feel tired - have a sore throat

13°C @ 0834 lightly Raining   Slept 1 hour during day
Overcast   Slept 7 1/4 hours   MILES/TIME

TUES.

DATE June 24

COURSE/NOTES Feel tired although less than yesterday.
Throat not as sore but have more head cold systems
such as a runny nose

12° @ 0740   Overcast   Slept 6 hours   MILES/TIME
Sunrise 0508   Sunset 2122   Sunshine/6:14 hours/minute

WED.

DATE June 25

COURSE/NOTES

15°C @ 1600   Overcast   Slept 6 1/2 hours   MILES/TIME

THUR.

DATE June 26

COURSE/NOTES

14°C @ 1008   Sunny with mostly   Slept 5 1/2 hours   MILES/TIME
cloudy

DATE June 27   **F**RI.

COURSE/NOTES _____
_____
_____
_____

Airport Chux
13°C @ 0742
12°C @ 0742   Over-cast   Slept 3½ hours
Downtown   MILES/TIME

DATE June 28   **S**AT.

COURSE/NOTES _____
_____
_____
_____
_____

          Sunny   Slept   2¼ hours
                                            MILES/TIME

DATE June 29   **S**UN.

COURSE/NOTES Run with Graeme & Vince
_____
_____
_____
                                            Jazz 189.4
                                            20M
14°C @ 0602   Overcast   Slept 6 hours   1:55.43
Sunrise 0514 Sunset 2122 Sunshine 16:11   MILES/TIME

                                                REVIEW

GOALS/NOTES _____
_____
_____
_____
_____

WEIGHT   CUMULATIVE   505.4   WEEKLY   20 . M
                     TOTAL   207·35   TOTAL
                                              Run 485.4 M
                                              Bike 207.35 M

MON.

DATE June 30

COURSE/NOTES _____

_____

_____

_____

_____

11°C @ 0700 Partly Cloudy Slept 8 3/4 hours _____ MILES/TIME

TUES.

DATE July 1

COURSE/NOTES Ran around Burnaby Lake with Graeme
and Vince

_____

_____

_____

	123 516.6km
	52:25:59
	10.6k

13°C @ 0646   Raining   Slept 7 1/4 hours MILES/TIME

Sunrise 0512   Sunset 2121   Sunshine 16:09

WED.

DATE July 2

COURSE/NOTES _____

_____

_____

_____

weather channel Sunny with

13°C @ 0629 Some high thin cloud Slept 6 3/4 hours MILES/TIME

THUR.

DATE July 3

COURSE/NOTES _____

_____

_____

_____

15°C Downtown at lunx

14°C @ 0651   Sunny with some   Slept 5 3/4 hours MILES/TIME

Weight 137 lbs   high thin cloud

DATE _July 4_   **FRI.**

COURSE/NOTES _Ran with Graeme from his health club around sea_
wall counter clockwise through English Bay to under Granville St
Bridge. warm up   1st mile   2nd mile 7.46.10, 3 mile
7.41.31, 4th mile 7.44.91, 5th mile 7.46.57, 6th mile 7.40.53
7th mile 7.23.35 Cool down 2.8.30.82. 1/2 or 3/8 mile
+ warm up 38.25.39 Total 1:29.46

JAS 205.4
Towles 16k
1:29.46

13°C @ 0548 Sunny high thin cloud slept 6 1/4 hours   MILES/TIME

DATE _July 5_   **SAT.**

COURSE/NOTES _____
_____
_____
_____

Weather Channel
18°C @ 0906 Thunder Lightening slept 9 1/4 hours!   MILES/TIME
Sunrise 0515 Sunset 2120   Sundnew 16:05

DATE _July 6_   **SUN.**

COURSE/NOTES _Ran O Avenue in South Surrey and Langley_
with Graeme and Bruce 13.6 miles
_____
_____

Weather Channel
16°C @ 0624   Overcast   slept 6 1/2 hours   MILES/TIME

125134.01
21.76k
1:55.21

REVIEW

GOALS/NOTES _____
_____
_____
_____
_____

WEIGHT [ ]   CUMULATIVE TOTAL | 553.76 | WEEKLY TOTAL | 48.36M |
           cycle 207.35k
                                      Run 505.4
                                      Bike 207.35k

MON.

DATE _July 7_

COURSE/NOTES _____

_____

_____

_____

_____

CBC
15°C @ 0745   Overcast Slept 7 hours   MILES/TIME

TUES.

DATE _July 8_

COURSE/NOTES _Ran Stanley Park trails with Graeme_
≈ 9 - 9.5km

Weather Channel   Shadow II 107k
15°C @ 0530   Raining Slept 7 1/4 hours   MILES/TIME   56.57.67
Sunrise 0517 Sunset 2118 Sunshine 16:01   9h

WED.

DATE _July 9_

COURSE/NOTES _____

_____

_____

_____

Weather Channel   Both
15°C @ 0734   Sunny/Cloudy Slept 7 hours   MILES/TIME
Sunrise 0518 Sunset 2117 Sunshine 15:59

THUR.

DATE _July 10_

COURSE/NOTES _____

_____

_____

_____

_____

CKWX Downtown
12°C @ 0551   Raining   Slept 7 3/4 hours   MILES/TIME

DATE July 11   **F**RI.

COURSE/NOTES _____
_____
_____
_____
_____
_____

16°C @ 0952 Mostly cloudy Slept 7hours MILES/TIME

DATE July 12   **S**AT.

COURSE/NOTES _____
_____
_____
_____
_____

weather channel
19°C @ 1233 Overcast   Slept 6½hours MILES/TIME

DATE July 13   **S**UN.

COURSE/NOTES Did Grouse Grind with Liliane Harf
53.39.31 to wire in rock
_____
_____

Downtown Chux   Alfresco 25k
14°C @ 0723 Some high thin cloud   ≥14
12°C @ 0723 Mostly sunny   Slept   MILES/TIME   53.39.31
Airport

                                                      REVIEW

GOALS/NOTES _____
_____
_____
_____
_____

WEIGHT   CUMULATIVE   563.76   WEEKLY   110.36.98
                TOTAL   TOTAL   10k
                             207.35   553.76M
                                                207.35k

Above: Leaders of the second leg of the college women's 4 x 1,500 meter relay, 1993 Penn Relays. Right: William Sigei on his way to winning the 1993 Cross Country World Championships, Amorebieta, Spain.

"Start everyday off with a smile and get it over with."

-W.C. Fields

Gina Procacio in the 1992 Freihofer 5 kilometer road race.

"The biggest sin is sitting on your ass."

-Florynce Kennedy

MON.

COURSE/NOTES _____

_____
_____
_____
_____

CKWR
16°C Downtown   Sunny
17°C Airport @ 0642 Mostly Cloudy Slept 6¾ hour   MILES/TIME
Sunrise 0523   Sunset 2114   Sunshine 15:51

TUES.

DATE July 15

COURSE/NOTES Ran over to Baladava Park and around
track 8 times then home
    Run 34.27.53   walk 11.21.24
400 meters 1.32.68   400 meters 1.36.94   800 3.09.53   6.18.03 /mi
800 meters 3.35.55   7.11.10 mile
                                                    Shadow # 113k
weather channel   34.27.53
15°C @ 0701   Overcast   Slept 7½ hours   MILES/TIME 5.5k
Sunrise 0524 Sunset 2113   Sunshine 15:49

WED.

DATE July 16

COURSE/NOTES _____

_____
_____
_____
_____

Weather Channel Some high blue cloud
15°C @ 0650 Sunny! Slept 6¼ hours   MILES/TIME
Sunrise 0525 Set 2112   Sunshine 15:47

THUR.

DATE July 17

COURSE/NOTES _____

_____
_____
_____
_____

weather channel
17°C @ 0756 Overcast   Slept 7 hours   MILES/TIME

DATE _July 18_   **F**RI.

COURSE/NOTES _____
_____
_____
_____

weather channel
14°c @ 0705   Sunny! Slept 7¼ hours   MILES/TIME
Sunrise 0527   Sunset 2110 Sunshine 15:43

DATE _July 19_   **S**AT.

                Ran sea wall with Graeme
COURSE/NOTES
went to whistler
_____
_____

                                            Shadow II 22.5k
Downtown CKWX   9.5k
14°c @ 0612   Sunny   Slept 6 hours   MILES/TIME   1:05.1

DATE _July 20_   **S**UN.

            at Whistler   Rode bike
COURSE/NOTES
Up to 900°F on shannon's thermometer
Road some of valley trail from Alta Lake to Village
Great trail!
_____

Shannon's Thermometer   49.30
12°c @ 0751   Sunny   Slept 6 hours   MILES/TIME   Ride 14.06k

                                                        REVIEW

GOALS/NOTES _____
_____
_____
_____

                        14.06 Bike   14.06 Bike
                        15 k running   15 k
WEIGHT   CUMULATIVE T 2:30.07   WEEKLY   T 2:30.07
            TOTAL   Run 578.76   TOTAL   563.76
                        Bike 221.41   207.35

MON.

COURSE/NOTES at Whistler

Shannon's Thermometer Sunny
15°C @ 0824 some thin
high clouds   Slept 7 hours   MILES/TIME

TUES.

COURSE/NOTES at Whistler
- Outside left foot sore upon rising but went away
during day
Rode bike on Valley Trail to Lost Lake to Green lake
to Recreation centre back along Valley Trail   AVS 18.0 km/hour
to Shannon's.   MXS 49.5 km/hour
Shannon's Thermometer   1.16.41
10°C @ 0829 Raining lightly Slept 9½ hours   23.14 k
                                    MILES/TIME

WED.

COURSE/NOTES at Whistler
- Outside left foot sore upon rising

Shannon's Thermometer some sun
10°C @ 0841 Mostly Cloudy   Slept 7½ hours   MILES/TIME

THUR.

COURSE/NOTES at Whistler morning/afternoon Returned to Vancouver evening
- No pain in left foot upon rising or otherwise!
Rode bike at Whistler Bike Park

10°C @ 0841 Partly cloudy Sunny Slept 7 hours   MILES/TIME   16.41 k

DATE _July 25_ **FRI.**

COURSE/NOTES _____

CBC
16°C @ 0812   Sunny with some clouds   Slept 7 hours   MILES/TIME

DATE _July 26_ **SAT.**

COURSE/NOTES Fraser River - Saint Georges - Home trail
5.00.42 walk, 32.26.48 to 41st Ave, 36.53.88 to trail
sign 51.08.50 to Dunbar St, 1:06.12' to finish 7.00.56
cool down.

15°C Airport 0823   Stanley II 134 toh
Downtown chwx   1:06.12
17°C @ 0807   Mostly Cloudy   Slept 8½ hours   11.50h
Sunrise 0537   Sunset 2100 / Sunshine 15:23   MILES/TIME

DATE _July 27_ **SUN.**

COURSE/NOTES Ran with Graeme, Vince & Kim   Jow   start at 1550 Alberni
Stanley Park Sea wall counter clockwise under Granville St. bridge
around False creek to planetarium to Kitsilano concession
start back over Burrard bridge to Pacific, North on
Cardero to Alberni start   30.22.30 from 2k to 8k
Downtown & Airport chwx   Avg 125 160.01
14°C @ 0552   Sunny   Slept 4¾ hours   2:21.35
                                        MILES/TIME   26k

REVIEW

GOALS/NOTES _____

WEIGHT 136 lbs   CUMULATIVE TOTAL 616.26   WEEKLY TOTAL Bike 37.55
                                                            3:27.47
                                                            37.5h
                                                            578.76
                                                            221.41

Bike 260.96

MON.
DATE July 28

COURSE/NOTES _____

We
17°C @ 0850   Sunny   Slept 8 hours   MILES/TIME
Sunrise 0540 Sunset 2058

TUES.
DATE July 29

COURSE/NOTES _____

Vancouver
Weather Channel   Sunny
16°C @ 0727   A few clouds Slept 7 hours   MILES/TIME
Sunrise 0541 Sunset 2056 Sunshine 5:15

WED.
DATE July 30

COURSE/NOTES Victoria
Walked with Susan in regular blue buggy west along
Seaward for 1 mile then came back same route

                                                    Jazz 207.4 k
                                           slept 6   Walked 46 min
            Sunny Some Cloud in East   MILES/TIME 2 miles

THUR.
DATE July 31

COURSE/NOTES Victoria
Walked into Downtown Victoria around legislature over
to Provincial Museum over to Beacon Hill park then
back to Hotel along Government St.

                                                    Jazz 216.4 k
                                                    Walked
            Sunny   slept 5 1/2 hours MILES/TIME 2015 ~9k

DATE ~~■■■~~ Aug 1   **FRI.**

COURSE/NOTES Victoria

_____

27°C @ 1400 sunny   Slept 9hours   MILES/TIME

DATE Aug 2   **SAT.**

COURSE/NOTES _____

Downtown 16°C at Airport
18°C @ 0800 CFWX Cloudy
Weather Channel
16°C @ 0730   Overcast   Slept 6½ hours   MILES/TIME
Sunrise 0547 Sunset 2050 Sunshine 15:03

DATE Aug 3   **SUN.**

COURSE/NOTES Run from Ambleside beach to Cleveland Dam to
bottom of Grouse Grind then up Grouse Grind. 3700 Vertical feet
Cycle with Bruce Law easy through UBC trails
Lap1 40.43.53 Capilano Dam Lap2 13.20.51 Capilano Dam
to Grouse Grind Pause for 57.91 Grouse Grind 52.41.37
Total 1:46.55 Grouse Grind 2.7K   1:24.2 Ride 17.19K
Weather channel   1:46.55
16°C @ 0542   Sunny   Slept 5¼ hours   MILES/TIME Run 7.7K
Sunrise 0548 Sunset 2049 Sunshine 15:01   Jazz 23

REVIEW

GOALS/NOTES _____

| WEIGHT | CUMULATIVE TOTAL | 623.96 | WEEKLY TOTAL | 3:10.75 B17.19k R7.7k |
| | Bike | 278.15 | | Run 616.26 Bike 260.96 |

MON.
DATE Aug. 4

COURSE/NOTES Sore lower back from biking incident, where the front of the seat hit my lower back.

18°C @ 0853   Sunny   Slept 8½ hours   MILES/TIME

TUES.
DATE Aug. 5

COURSE/NOTES

16°C @ 0640   Sunny   slept 6¼ hours   MILES/TIME
Sunrise 0551   Sunset 2046   Sunshine: 14:54

WED.
DATE Aug. 6

COURSE/NOTES "New" course walk 5.10.38   41st Ave 31.31.83
Trail sign 35:59.42   4.27.49   Trail sign 56 Georges School
43.10.42   7.11.0   Danbas St 49.26.97   6.16.55
Finish 1:03.07   13.40.13   Cool down walk 6.27.70
* Storm lightning thunder @ 1130 to 1330
17° Downtown   Shadow II 135.56
Airport clear   1:03.07
18° @ 0531   Mostly clear some clouds slept 6 hours   MILES/TIME   11.5/1
Sunrise 0552   Sunset 2044   14:52

THUR.
DATE Aug. 7

COURSE/NOTES

15°C @ Downtown
16°C @ 0621   Overcast   slept 6½ hours   MILES/TIME
Airport   Sunrise 0553   Sunset 2042   Sunshine 14:49

DATE _Aug. 8_ **FRI.**

COURSE/NOTES _Left shin mid section outside of large_
Bone   feels sore!
Ran Graeme's Health Club route with Graeme Clockwise
Weight on Graeme's Health Club scale 141½ with running
shoes and shorts shirt and socks on. At home 138 After running
clear   Shadow II 49.25
Airport and Downtown   1:02.50
13°C @ 0542 Clear   Slept 6 hours MILES/TIME   11.75 K

DATE _Aug. 9_ **SAT.**

COURSE/NOTES _____

_____

_____

_____

Airport Weather Channel
17°C @ 0730   Sunny   Slept 6½ hours MILES/TIME
Sunrise 0556   Sunset 2039/ Sunshine 14.43

DATE _Aug. 10_ **SUN.**

COURSE/NOTES _____

_____

29° Humidex
27° @ 0630
28°C Humidex   Shadow II 56.75
25°C @ 0823   8.5K
20°C @ 0830   Sunny   Slept 7¾ hours MILES/TIME   46.54.74

REVIEW

GOALS/NOTES _____

_____

_____

_____

_____

WEIGHT	CUMULATIVE TOTAL Run 655.71	WEEKLY TOTAL 2.52.1 / 31.75A
	Bike 278.15	Run 623.96 Bike 278.16

MON.
DATE Aug. 11

COURSE/NOTES _____

16°C @ 0712   Sunny.   Slept 6½ hours   MILES/TIME

TUES.
DATE Aug. 12

COURSE/NOTES _____

17°C Downtown Clear   shadow II / 68.25
17°C @ 0542   Clear   Slept 6¾ hours   MILES/TIME   1.5k   1:05.26

WED.
DATE Aug. 13

COURSE/NOTES Elm St to Trafalgar to W 31st to track at
Balaclava Park back to home along Carnarvon to
bath 05.10.31 Run 8.22.30 Lap 1 on track 2.05.52 Lap 2 1.38.17
Lap 3 2.18.76 Lap 4 2.10.30 Lap 5 1.41.26 Lap 6 2.14.62
Run to home 9.13.52 cool down = 6.00

17°C Downtown Clear   N.B. 110 4.6k
19°C Airport @ 0652 Sunny Slept 7¾ hours   MILES/TIME   34.54.84   4.6k.

THUR.
DATE Aug. 14

COURSE/NOTES _____

weather channel
16° @ 0722   Sunny   Slept 7¼ hours   MILES/TIME
Sunset 0603 Sunrise 2030 Sunshine 14:27

DATE Aug 15   **F**RI.

R

COURSE/NOTES Summerfast 10k   Hot! My running clothes have
never been so soaked with sweat! Official time 43.27
Last year 43.36. Vince start this year 43.12
1st mile 6.33.46   Between 1st and last mile 30.16.90
5k ± 21.10   last mile ± 6.36.65   7min/mile pace
16°C Downtown   Mostly Cloudy   NB110 Race 10k
Airport Chwx   Mixed Cloud
17°C at 0642   With Sun   Slept 7 hours   MILES/TIME | 43.27 10k |
Sunrise 0605   Sunset 2028   Sunshine 14:23   NB110 Total 14.5k

---

DATE Aug. 16   **S**AT.

COURSE/NOTES _____

26°C Downtown
Airport chwx Some
23°C @ 0852   Sunny   Slept 7 hours   MILES/TIME

DATE Aug. 17   **S**UN.

COURSE/NOTES Right Arm sore in morning upon rising
went to hospital @ 1630. Had surgery on right elbow.
Intravenous installed in left arm

Downtown Chwx
27°C @ 1012   Sunny   Slept 7½ hours   MILES/TIME

REVIEW

GOALS/NOTES _____

WEIGHT | CUMULATIVE TOTAL | 681.81 | WEEKLY TOTAL | 2.23.07 26.1
      Bik 278.15   Run 655.71
                        Bike 278.15

MON.
DATE Aug. 18

COURSE/NOTES Right arm in bandage   Attended hospital @ 1630

~~████████~~
17°C @ 0815 Sunny with some slept 8½ hours MILES/TIME
high cloud

TUES.
DATE Aug. 19

COURSE/NOTES Right arm in bandage. Went to hospital @ 1630

Downtown
20°C @ 0822 chwx Weather Channel
16°C @ 0815 Sunny   Slept 8½ hours MILES/TIME
Sunrise 0611   Sunset 2021   Sunshine 14:10

WED.
DATE Aug. 20

COURSE/NOTES Right arm hurts below (towards wrist) the elbow!
went to hospital @ 1630
Arm slightly itchy in afternoon
Intravenous removed from left arm.

Weather Channel
17°C @ 0750 Partly Cloudy   Slept 9 hours MILES/TIME
Sunrise 0612   Sunset 2019   Sunshine 14:07

THUR.
DATE Aug. 21

COURSE/NOTES Right arm in bandage. Right arm tingling
or itchy some times during the day.

0721 chwx
15° Downtown
16° Airport   Overcast   Slept 8½ hours MILES/TIME
Sunrise 0613   Sunset 2017   Sunlight 14:04

DATE _Aug 22_ **F**RI.

COURSE/NOTES _____

Downtown CKWX
14°C @ 0737
Weather Channel
15°C @ 0734   Overcast Slept 7 hours   MILES/TIME
Sunrise 0615 Sunset 2015 Sunlight 14:00

DATE _Aug. 23_ **S**AT.

COURSE/NOTES _____

Downtown and Airport CKWX
16°C @ 0852 Overcast   Slept 8¼ hours   MILES/TIME
Sunrise 0616 Sunset 2013 Sunlight 13:57

DATE _Aug. 24_ **S**UN.

COURSE/NOTES _____

Downtown and Airport CKWX
15°C @ 0841 Overcast   Slept 9½ hours   MILES/TIME
Sunrise 0618 Sunset 2011 Sunlight 13:53

REVIEW

GOALS/NOTES _____

WEIGHT	CUMULATIVE TOTAL	0	WEEKLY TOTAL	0

Run 681.81
Bike 278.15

MON.

COURSE/NOTES _____

16°C Airport
Downtown Churr
15°C @ 0731   Raining   Slept 8 1/4 hours
MILES/TIME

TUES.

COURSE/NOTES Ran around False Creek over Burrard
Bridge, Past Indy Car Paddock back to Granville Island
with Graeme

Weather Channel A light brief sprinkle   Shadow 178.25
16°C @ 0550   Overcast   Slept 6 3/4 hours   51, 13.32
                          MILES/TIME   70H
Sunrise 0621 Sunset 2007 Sunlight 13:46

WED.

COURSE/NOTES _____

Weather Channel
15°C @ 0800   Overcast   Slept 8 3/4 hour
                          MILES/TIME
Sunrise 0622   Sunset 2005   sun 13:43
                              10y4

THUR.

COURSE/NOTES Shaughnessy 5K

Weather Channel   Shadow 185.4
15°C 0644   Overcast   Slept 7 1/2 hours   5K 23.41.31
                          MILES/TIME   7.2K 42.05.8
Sunrise 0624 Sunset 2003 Sunlight 13:39

DATE ___Aug 29___   **F**RI.

COURSE/NOTES __Around Stanley Park seawall clockwise__
__except a detour to Brockton Oval washroom__

Shadow # 195.95

	MILES/TIME	
13ºC Downtown		54.14.79
15ºC @ 0551 Overcast Slept 6½ hours		10.54
Sunrise 0625 Sunset 2001 Sunlight 13:36		

DATE ___Aug 30___   **S**AT.

COURSE/NOTES _____

	MILES/TIME	
15ºC Downtown		Asics 125 179.0
Airport 6kwh		1:41.18
17ºC @ 0551 Overcast Slept 7 hours		19M
135 lbs after run		

DATE ___Aug. 31___   **S**UN.

COURSE/NOTES _____

	MILES/TIME	
21ºC Airport		
5rw x		
23ºC @ 1700 Sunny Slept 6½ hours		

REVIEW

GOALS/NOTES _____

WEIGHT	CUMULATIVE TOTAL	727.51	WEEKLY TOTAL	4:08.5 46.7
		Bike 278.15	Run	681.81
			Bike	278.15

Above: Brad Sumner on the third leg of the winning men's 4 x 1,500 meter relay, 1993 Penn Relays. Right: Competitor in the 1990 New York Games women's 2,000 meter steeplechase.

"The greater the difficulty, the more glory in surmounting it."

-*Epicurus*

Competitor with less than a mile to go in the 1993 Los Angeles
Marathon, where it was a tough 85 ˚ on race day.

"There are some defeats more triumphant
than victories."

-Michel de Montaigne

MON.

COURSE/NOTES _____

18° Downtown   Some cloud
16° Airport @ 0752 Sunny   Slept 7½ hours   MILES/TIME
Sunrise 0630 Sunset 1955

TUES.

COURSE/NOTES _____

            Clear Some Clouds
15°C @ 0620 "Variable Clouds" Slept 6½ hours MILES/TIME
Sunrise 0631   Sunset 1953   Sunshine 13:22

WED.

COURSE/NOTES Ran "Park Trails" route with Graeme
_____

                                    Shadow II 207.45
weather Channel   1:00.26
14°C @ 0540 Some Cloud   slept 6 hours MILES/TIME 11.5K

THUR.

COURSE/NOTES Feeling tired!
_____

Humidity 94°
weather Channel Some cloud
13° @ 0644   Sunny   Slept 7 hours MILES/TIME
Sunrise 0634   Sunset 1947   Sunshine 13:15

DATE Sept. 5   **FRI.**

COURSE/NOTES _Feeling tired_
Graeme's Health Club around seawall counterclockwise
Lap 1 to mile 0 6.56.83, 3 miles 23,20.48 mile 4 7.30.63
mile 5 7.24.73 5 miles 38.15.84 return to mile 7.34.53

150C @ 0545 Weather Channel

Slept 7 1/4 hours   MILES/TIME | 59.46.17 |
                                 | 11.76K |

Shadow II 2192

DATE Sept 6   **SAT.**

COURSE/NOTES _____

11°C @ 0752 Sunny   Slept 8 1/2 hours MILES/TIME | ASICS125202.0 |
                                                      | 2395.09 |
                                                      | 23.5 |

DATE Sept. 7   **SUN.**

COURSE/NOTES _____

Sunny   Slept 5 hours   MILES/TIME | |

REVIEW

GOALS/NOTES _____

WEIGHT | | CUMULATIVE TOTAL | 773.75 | WEEKLY TOTAL | 4:05 |
                                                          | 46.75 |
                        Bike 278.15   Run 727.51
                                                     Bike 278.15

MON.

DATE _Sept. 8_

COURSE/NOTES _____

_____

_____

_____

_____

weather channel

12°C @ 0705 sunny   slept 8½ hours   MILES/TIME

Sunrise 0639   Sunset 1940   Sunlight 13:01

TUES.

DATE _Sept. 9_

COURSE/NOTES _"New" course to Fraser River_

31.32.63 to 4154. 4:31.76 36.04.39 to sign post

6.38.15 42.42.54 to St George's, 6.21.98 49.04.52

to Dunbar St 12.45.59 to home / 1:01.50 total

	√22 227.9
	1:01.50
	11.54

weather channel

14°C @ 0555 clear some clouds slept 7 hours   MILES/TIME

Sunrise 0644   Sunset 1938   Sunlight 12:57
        0641   12:57

WED.

DATE _Sept. 10_

COURSE/NOTES _Ran Seawall counter clockwise with Graeme_

_____

_____

_____

_____

	Shadow II 230.95
	1:04.26
	11.754

15°C @ 0533 Partly cloudy slept 5 hours   MILES/TIME

Sunrise 0642   Sunset 1936

THUR.

DATE _Sept. 11_

COURSE/NOTES (See Friday Sept. 12)

_____

_____

_____

_____

17°C @ 0554   slept 6¼ hours   MILES/TIME

Sunrise 0644   Sunset 1934   Sunlight 12:50

DATE ___Sept.12___ ⌐Sept. 11 **FRI.**

COURSE/NOTES ___Newest course - variation on new___
course - house to 41st to Blenheim to Fraser River
then usual new course. 33.53.36 to 41st
5.06.84 to spyh post 39.00.21, 8.09.75 47.08.85
to St. Georges sigh post, 6.25.18, 53.35.13 to
to Danba st 13.23.72 to home)   Jazz 239.4
to home   11.5K
120C Downtown ck wx Overcast   1:06.58
130C @ 0737 Airport   Slept 9 hours   **MILES/TIME**
Sunrise 0645 Sunset 1932 Sunlight 12:47

DATE ___Sept.13___ **SAT.**

COURSE/NOTES _____
_____
_____
_____

130C Downtown
Airport ck wx Mostly Sunny
120C @ 0738 Some high thin cloud Slept 9½ hours **MILES/TIME**

DATE ___Sept.14___ **SUN.**

COURSE/NOTES _____
_____
_____
_____

120C Downtown   123 546.6
Airport ck wx   30H
140C @ 0612 Raining   Slept 6 hours **MILES/TIME** 2:55.42

REVIEW

GOALS/NOTES _____
_____
_____
_____
_____

WEIGHT [   ]   CUMULATIVE TOTAL 838.5   WEEKLY TOTAL 6:08.56
                        Bike 278.15   64.75H
                                           Run 773.75
                                           Bike 278.15

MON.

DATE Sept. 15

COURSE/NOTES _____
_____
_____
_____

14°C @ 0656   Raining Slept 8¾ hours
Sunrise 0649   Sunset 1925   Sunlight 12:36

MILES/TIME

TUES.

DATE Sept. 16

COURSE/NOTES Ran from Graeme's health club counter clockwise
around the seawall with Graeme.   mile 1 8.36.32
- Feel like I'm getting a sore throat 1/23 4.08.92
Feeling tired and run down 1/24 3.57.50 1/25 4.11.86
1/26 4.07.50 1/27 4.01.86, 1/28 4.06.50, 1/29 4.04.16
11°C Downtown 1/2 10 4.00.76   Shadow 12:42.7
Airport chinook   1:02.54.04
12°C @ 0551   Overcast   Slept 7 hours   11.75k
Sunrise 0651   Sunset 1923   Sunlight 12:32

MILES/TIME

WED.

DATE Sept. 17

COURSE/NOTES Feeling tired and like I'm getting sick - a cold.
_____
_____
_____

12° Downtown   Low 9.9   High 18.2
14° @ 0641 Airport Raining Slept 8¼ hours
Sunrise 0652   Sunset 1921   Sunlight 12:29

MILES/TIME

THUR.

DATE Sept. 18

COURSE/NOTES Feeling tired - still feeling like I'm getting sick
_____
_____
_____

             Some clouds in southern sky
12°C @ 0610 Mostly clear Slept 7¼ hours
Sunrise 0654   Sunset 1919   Sunlight 12:25
        Low 9.4   High 18.0

MILES/TIME

DATE Sept. 19   **F**RI.

COURSE/NOTES Still feeling like I'm fighting a cold

Humidity 100% low 9.8 high 17.5
Coldest morning since May 8!
9°C @ 0612   Clear   slept 6¾ hours   MILES/TIME
Sunrise 0655   Sunset 1907   Sunlight 12:22

DATE Sept. 20   **S**AT.

COURSE/NOTES Feel like I have a cold. My voice is hoarse

13°C @ 0757   Sunny   slept 8 hours   MILES/TIME
Sunrise ~~xxxx~~   Sunset 1914   Sunlight 12:17
       0657

DATE Sept. 21   **S**UN.

COURSE/NOTES Have a cold. Have a slight cough.
Coughing up phlegm. Feel better than Saturday.

                        Low 9.1 High 17.9
Humidity 100%
11°C @ 0821   Sunny   slept 8 hours   MILES/TIME
Sunrise 0658   Sunset 1912   Sunlight 12:14

                                                 REVIEW

GOALS/NOTES

WEIGHT   CUMULATIVE   850.25   WEEKLY   11.75
                  TOTAL   TOTAL
                        Ride 278.15   Run 838.5
                                                     Ride 278.15

MON.

Fall Equinox

DATE Sept. 22

COURSE/NOTES Still have a mild cold. Still coughing up phlem.

Fall begins at 1656

12°c Downtown ckwx Some high thin cloud
11°C @ 0723 Mostly clear Slept 6½ hours
Sunrise 0700 Sunset 1910 Day light 12:10

MILES/TIME

TUES.

DATE Sept. 23

COURSE/NOTES

13°c Downtown   9.2   19.6
Airport
13°C @ 0800 Sunny   Slept 8½ hours
Sunrise 0701 Sunset 1908 Day light 12:07

MILES/TIME

WED.

DATE Sept. 24

COURSE/NOTES Ran Seawall counter clockwise with Graeme
½ mile 1 > 3.49.25, 2: 3.59.24, 3: 3.52.18, 4: 3.49.04,
5: 4.05.30 6: 3.49.50, 7: 3.56.64, 8: 3.56.52, 9: 3.56.38,
10: 4.07.85 5 miles: 39.21.90

                                          Slow hours 254.45
                  Low 9.0   High 17.5   1:01.46.19
11°C @ 0530   Clear   Slept 5½ hours   11.75h
Sunrise 0702 Sunset 1906 Day light 12:04   MILES/TIME

THUR.

DATE Sept. 25

COURSE/NOTES Newest course start from home to 41st to Blenheim
to Celtic along Fraser River 1:30.45 to 3h 5.24.72 to 4th
4.52.26 to 9h 3.53.07 to 41st Ave 4.33.84 to 70st
7.16.08 to St Georges school 6.41.25 to Dunbar St
29.40.5 to 41st

                  Low 9.3 High 17.5   Jazz 250.9
                                             1:01.00
15°C @ 0636   Overcast   Slept 7¼ hours   11.5h
Sunrise 0704 Sunset 1904 Day light 12:00   MILES/TIME

DATE Sept. 26   **F**RI.

COURSE/NOTES _____

_____

_____

_____

11°C Downtown   Low 9.2   High 16.9

15°C @ 0649   Overcast   Slept 7 hours   MILES/TIME

Sunrise 0705   Sunset 1902   Daylight 11:57

DATE Sept. 27   **S**AT.

COURSE/NOTES Breakfast at Macdonald Realtors.
Received Call from Sno + Security @ 0255.

_____

_____

_____

                        Slept 5½ hour

Sunrise 070   Sunset 11   Daylight 11:   MILES/TIME

DATE Sept. 28   **S**UN.

COURSE/NOTES Seymour Forest ½ Marathon. The race
that had the most rain of any race to date

_____

T 20C Downtown   13°C Airport   CKWX   Asics 125 223 ol
weather Channel   Low 8.9   High 16.6   1.46.40
14°C @ 0651   Raining   Slept 7¾ hours   21.14
Sunrise 0708   Sunset 1857   Daylight 11:49   MILES/TIME

REVIEW

GOALS/NOTES _____

_____

_____

_____

_____

WEIGHT	CUMULATIVE TOTAL	894.60	WEEKLY TOTAL	3.4926 44.35h

Ride 278.15

Run 850.25
Rid 278.15

MON.

COURSE/NOTES

low 9.6 High 16.5
13°C @ 0605   Overcast   Slept 7 hours
Sunrise 0710   Sunset 1855   Sunlight 11:45

MILES/TIME

TUES.

COURSE/NOTES Ran sea wall Counter Clockwise with Graeme
1/2 mile 1: 4.47.16, 2: 4.28.98, 3: 4.22.56, 4: 4.16.65,
5: 4.16.29, 6: 4.17.66, 7: 4.18.34, 8: 4.07.66,
9: 3.55.69, 10: 3.50.40

15°C Downtown Low 9.5 High 16.8
16°C @ 0541 Raining Slept 6 1/2 hours
Sunrise 07 Sunset 18 Daylight 11:

Shadow II 266.2
1:05,26.7
11.25h

MILES/TIME

WED.

COURSE/NOTES Ran Park Trails slightly different course
with Graeme

OLWX Humidity 100%
11°C Downtown
12°C @ 0542 Raining 5 3/4 hours
Sunrise 0713 Sunset 1851 Daylight 11:38

Jazz 261.9
1:02.53
11.3k

MILES/TIME

THUR.

COURSE/NOTES

Low 7.9 High 16.4
13°C @ 0637 Light rain Slept 7 hours
Sunrise 0714 Sunset 1849 Daylight 11:35

MILES/TIME

DATE Oct.3   **F**RI.

COURSE/NOTES Ran Seawall Counterclockwise with Graeme
Felt like I had allergy problems with my nose.

Shadow II 277.95

59.13.91

11.75H

11°C @ 0531   Low 8.1   High 15.8
Sunrise 0716   Rainy/Dry   Slept 7 hours   MILES/TIME
   Sunset 1847   Daylight 11:31

DATE Oct.4   **S**AT.

COURSE/NOTES Felt like I had allergy problems all day

~~12°C Downtown~~ MILES/TIME
~~12°C @ 0531~~
Sunrise 07   Sunset 18   Slept 9 hours!
                   Daylight

DATE Oct.5   **S**UN.

COURSE/NOTES Felt tightness in chest area in area of
my heart around 30K. Felt pain on lateral
side of right knee - IT band!

Asics 125 258.6

3.24

35.5H

10°C Downtown Crux   Low 6.9   High 15.1
12°C @ 0531   Overcast   Slept 14 hours   MILES/TIME
Sunrise 0719   Sunset 1842   Daylight 11:23

REVIEW

GOALS/NOTES

WEIGHT   CUMULATIVE TOTAL   964.6   WEEKLY TOTAL   6:31.32 70K
Ride 278.15   Run 894.6
                       Ride 278.15

MON.

DATE Oct. 6

COURSE/NOTES My right lower outside knee area is sore

→ 9°C Downtown Low 7.4 High 15.4
→ 6°C @ 0712   Overcast Slept 7 3/4 hours   MILES/TIME
  Sunrise 0720 Sunset 1840 Sunlight 11:20

TUES.

DATE Oct. 7

COURSE/NOTES _te outside of my right leg just below
the knee still hurts.
Ran False Creek from Granville Island with Graeme

7°C Downtown   shadow 287.45
7°C @ 0530 Mostly Cloudy Slept 7 hours   MILES/TIME 53.22.5
Sunrise 0722 Sunset 1838   Sunlight 11:16   9.5h

WED.

DATE Oct. 8

COURSE/NOTES Snowing on Grouse Mountain according to CBC

7°C @ 0721 CKWX Downtown
10°C @ 0717 weather channel
CBC   Low 7.7   High 15.2
9°C @ 0715   Raining   Slept 6 1/4 hours   MILES/TIME
Sunrise 0723   Sunset 1836   Sunlight 11:13

THUR.

DATE Oct. 9

COURSE/NOTES

9° AVB Port CKWX
  Humidity 78%
8°C Downtown low 7.8 high 15.0
10°C @ 0520   Overcast   Slept 6 1/2 hours   MILES/TIME   Jazz 271.4
Sunrise 0725   Sunset 1834   Sunlight 11:09   46.57.48
                                                            9.5h

DATE _Oct. 10_   **FRI.**

COURSE/NOTES _Feel tired Sore lower back, knee (right outside
lower) I.T. band? not sore_

8°C Downtown low 7.7 high 15.0   Slow II 299.2
10°C @ 0551 Overcast Slept 6¾ hours   1:05.48
Sunrise 0726   Sunset 1832   Sunlight 11:06   **MILES/TIME** 11.5M 1:02.17.24

DATE _Oct. 11_   **SAT.**

COURSE/NOTES

8°C @ 0840   Sunny   Slept 4½ hours
Sunrise 0728   Sunset 1830   Sunlight 11:02   **MILES/TIME**

DATE _Oct. 12_   **SUN.**

COURSE/NOTES _Ran from 25 st in west Van to Cledans
Dam down Capilano road back to 25 st.
with Graeme and Vince Hart. Could feel I.T. band
on right leg on lateral side of right knee._

5°C Downtown CHUX Low 7.1 High 14.3   Jazz 289.9
6°C @ 0632 Overcast Slept 6 hours   1:44.09
Sunrise 0729   Sunset 1828   Sunlight 10:59   **MILES/TIME** 18.5M

REVIEW

GOALS/NOTES

WEIGHT   CUMULATIVE TOTAL _1013.85_   WEEKLY TOTAL _4:26.46.23_ _49.25 K_
                   Ride 278.15   Run 964.6
                                             Ride 278.15

MON.

COURSE/NOTES _____

100% @ 0731 Overcast Slept 8 hours | MILES/TIME

Sunrise 0731 Sunset 1826 Sunlight 10:55

TUES.

COURSE/NOTES _____

9°C Downtown Low 6.9 High 13.7
11°C @ 0650 Overcast Slept 7 hours | MILES/TIME

Sunrise 0732 Sunset 1824 Sunlight 10:52

WED.

COURSE/NOTES Ran Park trails in reverse ½ way to
Prospect Point and then the park road ⅓ dirt ⅔ Asphalt
Could feel IT Band on Right leg

Humidity 100%
9°C Downtown Low 6.0 High 14.0
11°C @ 0536 Raining Slept 6 hours | MILES/TIME

Sunrise 0734 Sunset 1822 Sunlight 10:48

Shadow II 310.7
≈ 1:05
≈ 11.5h

THUR.

COURSE/NOTES Ran False Creek Sea wall counter clockwise
with Graeme. Could feel IT Band on right side of right
knee

13°C Downtown Low 5.4 High 13.3
14°C @ 0550 Variable Clouds Slept 6¾ hours | MILES/TIME

Sunrise 0736 Sunset 1820 Starlight 10:44

∫azz 299.4
51:23.75
9.5h

DATE _Oct. 17_   **FRI.**

COURSE/NOTES   Do not feel IT Band on right knee
Iced IT band 2 times in morning and at around
2200.

10°C Downtown	Low 5.4	High 12.9
11°C @ 0649	Variable clouds slept 7 1/4 hours	
Sunrise 0737	Sunset 1818	Sunlight 10:41

MILES/TIME [ ]

DATE _Oct. 18_   **SAT.**

COURSE/NOTES   Do not feel IT Band on right knee upon
rising

Humidity 100%		
5°C Downtown	Low 5.9	High 12.8
5°C @ 0741	Some thin clouds slept 8 hours	
Sunrise 0738	Sunset 1816	Daylight 10:37

MILES/TIME [ ]

DATE _Oct. 19_   **SUN.**

COURSE/NOTES   Felt good psychologically whole run... day.
Could feel my IT band on right side during the run.
At end of run quads, calves and glutes very sore

4°C Downtown!	Low 6.3	High 13.0	NB 825/00.5
8°C @ 0534	A few clouds slept		3:58:19
Sunrise 0740	Sunset 1814	Daylight 10:34	41.5k

MILES/TIME

REVIEW

GOALS/NOTES _____

| WEIGHT | 146 lbs | CUMULATIVE TOTAL | 1,076.35 | WEEKLY TOTAL | 5:54:42 62.5k |

shoes   Oct. 15
on etc Graeme's health club scale
                    Ride 278.15

                                                    1,013.85
                                                    Ride 278.15

Above: Mary Slaney in the 1992 Olympic Trials 1,500 meter heat.
Right: High school teamates pass the baton in the 4 x 400 meter relay,
1993 Penn Relays.

"Only dead fish swim with the stream."

-Unknown

1992 Olympian Gwen Coogan in the 1993 World Cross Country Championships, Amorebieta, Spain.

"Never put off until tomorrow what you can do the day after tomorrow."

-Mark Twain

MON.

COURSE/NOTES Walk 10.01.18, Run (slowly) 10.00.60, walk 10.02.06. Felt stiff but later in the day felt (like the walk/run/walk was a benefit.) Felt sore in hip area outside of pelvis at top of leg on side of torso. Also felt like I had re-injured my right hip Sartorius as in July of '95

Humidity 100%
30℃ Downtown   low 6.3   high 12.7
-3℃ @ 0630   slept 7 1/4 hours
Sunrise 0742   Sunset 1812   Daylight 10:30

MILES/TIME

TUES.

COURSE/NOTES Sore high butt on both sides when getting up at 0430
Had a massage felt very good after

Humidity 100%
Snow high thin cloud Low 5.8 High 12.8
2℃ @ 0741 Mostly clear   Slept 5 hours
Sunrise 0743   Sunset 1811   Daylight 10:28

MILES/TIME

WED.

COURSE/NOTES Still sore in high butt area on both sides when getting up at 0620

7℃ Downtown @ 0637
8℃ Airport @ 0640x
Weather clearing   Low 5.8   High 12.3
9℃ @ 0625 Raining lightly slept 6 3/4 hours
Sunrise 0745   Sunset 1809   Daylight 10:24

MILES/TIME

THUR.

COURSE/NOTES Ran Seawall counterclockwise with Graeme
Could feel my IT Band on my right leg.

7℃ Downtown chux   Low 5.8   High 12.7
8℃ @ 0430 Variable clouds Slept 4 hours
Sunrise 0747   Sunset 1807   Daylight 10:20

Shadow 322.6
1:05.27.87
11.75h

MILES/TIME

DATE Oct. 24   **F**RI.

COURSE/NOTES _____

shadow 333.95
3°C Downtown   Low 6.1 High 12.8   1:00:23
4°C@ 0556   Clear   Slept 7hours   MILES/TIME 11.5 k
Sunrise 0748 Sunset 1805 Daylight 10:17

DATE Oct. 25   **S**AT.

COURSE/NOTES _____

7° Downtown 0712   Low 6.1 High 12.6
8°C@0703   Overcast   Slept 7hours MILES/TIME
Sunrise 0750   Sunset 1803   Daylight 10:13

DATE Oct. 26   **S**UN.

COURSE/NOTES _____

                    Low 5.5 High 12.1
10°C @0547 Overcast   Slept 6 3/4   MILES/TIME
Sunrise 0651 Sunset   1701   Daylight 10:10

REVIEW

GOALS/NOTES _____

WEIGHT [   ]   CUMULATIVE TOTAL [1,099.60]   WEEKLY TOTAL [2:05.0 23.25]
1,076.35
Ride 278.15

MON.

COURSE/NOTES

	Low 4.8	High 12.1	
9°C @ 0600	Overcast	slept 6 3/4	MILES/TIME
Sunrise 0653	Sunset 1700	Daylight 10:07	

TUES.

COURSE/NOTES Ran park trail up to Prospect Point
down around Beaver Lake then across to Brockton
Oval then back to Graeme's Health club with
Graeme. Could feel IT Band on right side.

Shadow ↗ 345.55

7°C Downtown	Low 5.0	High 11.9		1:06.24.58
9°C @ 0551	Overcast	slept 7 hours	MILES/TIME	11.6 h
Sunrise 0655	Sunset 1658	Daylight 10:03		

WED.

COURSE/NOTES Ran around False Creek with Graeme
IT Band did not hurt!

Shadow ↗ 355.25

7°C Downtown	Low 4.6	High 11.4		9.7 K?
10°C 0545	Overcast	slept 7 1/4 hours	MILES/TIME	47.03.5
Sunrise 0656	Sunset 1656	Daylight 10:00		

THUR.

COURSE/NOTES

	Low 5.1	High 11.3	
13°C @ 0600	clear	slept 6 hours	MILES/TIME
Sunrise 0658	Sunset 1654	Daylight 9:56	

DATE __Oct. 31__   **F**RI.

COURSE/NOTES _____
_____
_____
_____
_____

Low 5.4 High 11.5
10°C @ 0617 Variable Clouds Slept 6½ hours   MILES/TIME
Sunlight 0659 Sunset 1753 Daylight 9:54

DATE __Nov. 1__   **S**AT.

COURSE/NOTES __Rode bike to Steveston with Lorne__
_____
_____
_____
_____

Low 4.3 High 11.3   4:15
7°C @ 0710 Variable Clouds Slept 6 hours   MILES/TIME   71 K
Sunlight 0701 Sunset 1751 Daylight 9:50

DATE __Nov. 2__   **S**UN.

COURSE/NOTES _____
_____
_____
_____
_____

7°C Downtown Low 4.2 High 11.1
9°C @ 0551 Variable Clouds   Slept 6¾ hours   MILES/TIME
Sunlight 0703 Sunset 1649 Daylight 9:46

                                                        REVIEW

GOALS/NOTES _____
_____
_____
_____
_____
_____

WEIGHT   CUMULATIVE   WEEKLY   1:48.27
                  TOTAL   1,120.9   TOTAL   21.3
                        Ride 349.15   1,099.6
                                                 Ride 278.15

MON.

DATE Nov. 3

COURSE/NOTES _____

Low 5.0   High 11.2

11°C @ 0613 Raining   Slept 7 hours   **MILES/TIME**

Sunrise 0704   Sunset 1648   Daylight 9:44

TUES.

DATE Nov. 4

COURSE/NOTES Ran 41st to Blenheim to Celtic

3ʰ 15.29.93   4ᵏ 20.51.78   5.21.8   5ʰ 26.18.94   5.27.16
41st 30.04.91   trail post 34.36.07   St Georges 41.55.8
Dunbar 48.07.53   Shadows 366.75
6°C Downtown   Low 4.5 High 11.2   1:00.40
7°C @ 0551 Mostly Clear slept 6¾ hours   11.5k
                                      MILES/TIME
Sunrise 0706 Sunset 1646 Daylight 9:40

WED.

DATE Nov. 5

COURSE/NOTES Shaughnessy 8k plus 9 laps of Pt. Grey track
Fast lap 1 1.37.18   Fast lap 2 1.37.98,   Fast lap 3 1.37.50
Fast lap 4 1.33.53

                                                    Jazz 310.1 k
10°C Downtown   Low 3.9   High 10.6   57.16.4
11°C @ 0616   Overcast   slept 7 hours   10.7 k
                                      MILES/TIME
Sunrise 0707   Sunset 1645   Daylight 9:38

THUR.

DATE Nov. 6

COURSE/NOTES Ran to Balaclava park around track 8
times and back

                                                  Shadows 371.95
11°C Downtown   Low   High   5.2 k
13°C @ 0530   Raining   slept 8 hours   40.36
                                      MILES/TIME
Sunrise 0709   Sunset 1643   Daylight 9:34

DATE _Nov. 7_ **F**RI.

COURSE/NOTES _Feeling stressed by work_

Low 4.1   High 10.5
10°C @ 0647   Overcast   Slept 7¼ hours   MILES/TIME
Sunrise 0711   Sunset 1642   Daylight 9:31

DATE _Nov. 8_ **S**AT.

COURSE/NOTES _Feeling stressed out by work_

5°C Downtown   Low 3.9   High 9.8
8°C @ 0539   Fog   Slept 5½ hours   MILES/TIME
Sunrise 0712   Sunset 1640   Daylight 9:28

DATE _Nov. 9_ **S**UN.

COURSE/NOTES _Ran with Graeme and Kim Jow. Ran from
Planetarium counterclockwise around False creek
along sea wall to 3rd beach then up park trail
to Prospect Point down to Brockton out to mile 0
then along the seawall along Beach Ave over the
Burrard St. bridge and back to the Planetarium. Jazz 340._

3:50.84
~30k

30°C @ 0613   Clear   Slept 7¼ hours   MILES/TIME
Sunrise 0714   Sunset 1639   Daylight 9:25

REVIEW

GOALS/NOTES

WEIGHT	CUMULATIVE TOTAL	1178.3	WEEKLY TOTAL	5:29.26 57.4k
		Ride 349.15		1,120.9 Ride 349.15

MON.

DATE Nov.10

COURSE/NOTES: Walk 10 minutes 10.07.52 Run 5.07.97,
Walk 4.07.27 Run 5.11.69 Walk 7.50.30

2°C Downtown   Low 3.9 high 10.8
3°C @ 0632   Slept
Sunrise 0716 Sunset 1637   Daylight 9:21

Shackr? 375.95
32.18.14
4h

MILES/TIME

TUES.

DATE Nov.11

COURSE/NOTES: Rode with Lorne to Iona sewage plant
and back to my house

1°C @ 0729   Low 3.6 High 8.5
Variable Cloud Slept 5 1/2 hours   Ride 32.63 ?
Sunrise 0717 Sunset 1636 Daylight 9:19

MILES/TIME

WED.

DATE Nov.12

COURSE/NOTES

0°C Downtown   Low 3.3 High 8.3
0°C @ 0545   Slept 7 hours
Sunrise 0719 Sunset 1635   Daylight 9:16

MILES/TIME

THUR.

DATE Nov.13

COURSE/NOTES New Orleans

MILES/TIME

DATE _Nov. 14_ **F**RI.

COURSE/NOTES _New Orleans_

MILES/TIME

DATE _Nov. 15_ **S**AT.

COURSE/NOTES _New Orleans_

MILES/TIME

DATE _Nov. 16_ **S**UN.

COURSE/NOTES _New Orleans_

MILES/TIME

REVIEW

GOALS/NOTES

WEIGHT	CUMULATIVE TOTAL	WEEKLY TOTAL
	1182.3	4k
	Ride 381.78	1178.3
		349.15

MON.

DATE _Nov. 17_

COURSE/NOTES _Ran out and back on New Orleans along St. Charles St._

MILES/TIME

Azz 350.1
1:02.15
10h

TUES.

DATE _Nov. 18_

COURSE/NOTES _New Orleans returned to Vancouver at 2345_

54°C @ ×1500 Overcast   Slept 5½ hours   MILES/TIME

WED.

DATE _Nov. 19_

COURSE/NOTES

8°C @ 0714   ~~Low 2.3 High 8.7~~   MILES/TIME
~~Sunrise 0731 Overcast Slept 8 hours~~
~~Sunrise 0731 Sunset 1625 Daylight 8.54~~

THUR.

DATE _Nov. 20_

COURSE/NOTES

8°C @ 0714   Low 2.3 High 8.7   MILES/TIME
Sunrise 0731 Sunset 1625 Overcast Slept 8 hours
Daylight 8:54

DATE _Nov. 21_ **F**RI.

COURSE/NOTES _____

5°C Downtown   Low 1.5 High 8.1   Shadow II 384.95
6°C @ 0531   Slept 6½ hours   49.32.97
                                    MILES/TIME   ~9K
Sunrise 07:33 Sunset 1624 Daylight 8:51

DATE _Nov. 22_ **S**AT.

COURSE/NOTES _____

                Low 1.50 High 8.0
2°C @ 0645   Overcast   Slept 7 hours
                                    MILES/TIME
Sunrise 0734 Sunset 1624 Daylight 8:50

DATE _Nov. 23_ **S**UN.

COURSE/NOTES _____

8°C Downtown CKWX @ 0652
9°C Airport CKWX   Jazz 355.1
Weather Channel   Low 1.9 High 7.9   1:16.01
11°C @ 0641   Raining   Slept 7¾ hours   ~15K
                                    MILES/TIME
Sunrise 0736 Sunset 1623 Daylight 8:47

REVIEW

GOALS/NOTES _____

WEIGHT [ ]   CUMULATIVE TOTAL 1,216.3   WEEKLY TOTAL 34K
                                381.78   1182.3
                                                          381.78

MON.

DATE _Nov. 24_

COURSE/NOTES _____

6°C Downtown Low 2.4, High 8.3
9°C @ 0642 Partly Cloudy/Clear Slept 6 1/4   MILES/TIME
Sunrise 0737 Sunset 1622 Daylight 8:45

TUES.

DATE _Nov. 25_

COURSE/NOTES walk 1.1k 12.45 Run 5k 25.55.8
walk @ 1.1k > 12.45 Run stragegnerry 5k with
Graeme 1k 6.02.42, 2k 5.20.58 3k 5.00.13
4k 4.53.98 5k 4.38.15

-10°C (wind chill)!   5k done 372.15
3°C Downtown   Low 2.0 High 7.8   25.55.80
5°C @ 0628   Slept 6 1/2 hour   5k   MILES/TIME
Sunrise 0739 Sunset 1621 Daylight 8:42

WED.

DATE _Nov. 26_

COURSE/NOTES _____

                    Low 1.5 High 7.5
5°C @ 0711 Overcast   Slept 8 1/4 hours!   MILES/TIME
Sunrise 0740 Sunset 1640 Daylight 8:40

THUR.

DATE _Nov. 27_

COURSE/NOTES _____

                    Low 1.7 High 7.6
6°C @ 0601 Overcast   Slept 6 3/4   MILES/TIME
Sunrise 0741 Sunset 1619 Daylight 8:38

DATE _Nov. 28_   **FRI.**

COURSE/NOTES Slept from 2320 to 0530 then was
awake for a while then went back to sleep until
0730

                    Low 1.4   High 7.3
10°@ 0754   Rainy windy   Slept 7¼ hours   [ ] MILES/TIME
Sunrise 0743 Sunset 1619   Daylight 8:36

DATE _Nov. 29_   **S**AT.

COURSE/NOTES Seattle Marathon. Disappointing result!
The most painful side stitch on my left side at the
bottom of my rib cage between mile 15 and 16. It prevented
me from running. At mile 22 my left IT band went
sore suddenly. Shortly after both my knees were so sore
that I could not run.   Jazz 397.3
                                               4:35.03 my watch
46°C @ 0730   Rainy   Slept 4¾ hours MILES/TIME 42.2 K
Sunrise   Sunset   Daylight

DATE _Nov. 30_   **SUN.**

COURSE/NOTES

44°F @ 0810   Overcast   Slept 8¼ MILES/TIME
Sunrise   Sunset 16   Daylight

                                                    REVIEW

GOALS/NOTES

WEIGHT [ ]   CUMULATIVE TOTAL | 1,263.5 | WEEKLY TOTAL | 47.2 |
                      Ride 381.78   Run 1,216.3
                                            Ride 381.78

MON.

DATE Dec. 1

COURSE/NOTES Quads sore IT band on ~~left~~ right leg
sore

Mon 2.1 Max 9.1

4°C Downtown Low 2.5 High 7.8
6°C @ 0609 Variable Clouds Slept 6 3/4
Sunrise 0747 Sunset 1617 Daylight 8:30

MILES/TIME

TUES.

DATE Dec. 2

COURSE/NOTES Want to massage session with
Tori Mitchell

Min -1.4 Max 8.0

0°C Downtown! Low 2.8 High 7.9
-1°C @ 0531 Slept 5 3/4 hours
Sunrise 0748 Sunset 1617 Daylight 8:29

MILES/TIME

WED.

DATE Dec. 3

COURSE/NOTES Stretching and strengthening

Min 1.5 max 9.2
Low 2.9 High 8.1
0°C @ 0634 A few clouds Slept 7 1/4 hours
Sunrise 0749 Sunset 1616 Daylight 8:27

MILES/TIME

THUR.

DATE Dec. 4

COURSE/NOTES Stretching and strengthening

Min 1.1 Max 8.8
Low 1.6 High 7.6
2°C @ 0634 A few clouds Slept 7 1/4 hours
Sunrise 0750 Sunset 1616 Daylight 8:26

MILES/TIME

DATE Dec. 5   **F**RI.

COURSE/NOTES _____

Low 1.7 High 7.0
10°C@0630 A few clouds Slept 7 hours | MILES/TIME |
Sunrise 0752 Sunset 1615 Daylight 8:23

DATE Dec. 6   **S**AT.

COURSE/NOTES _____

Min 0 Max 5.5
Slept 7 hours | MILES/TIME |
Sunrise 0753? Sunset 1615 Daylight 8:22

DATE Dec. 7   **S**UN.

COURSE/NOTES _____

Min 0.3 Max 8.4
Low High
3°C@0823 Variable cloudy 7.34 | MILES/TIME |
Sunrise 0754 Sunset 1615 Daylight 8:21

REVIEW

GOALS/NOTES _____

| WEIGHT | | CUMULATIVE TOTAL | | WEEKLY TOTAL | |

Run 1263.5
Ride 386.78

Above: Delmir Dos Santos wins the 1993 San Blas Half Marathon, San Blas, Puerto Rico. Right: Lynn Jennings on her way to finishing third at the 1993 World Cross Country Championships, Amorebieta, Spain.

"There is no cure for birth and death save to enjoy the interval between."

-George Santayana

Kenya's junior men's team on their way to winning the top four places in the 1993 World Cross Country Championships, Amorebieta, Spain.

"There are days it takes all you have just to keep up with the losers."

-Robert Orben

MON.

COURSE/NOTES Stuff in lower back - upper butt
stretching and strengthing

7°C @ 0607 weather channel Min   Max
3°C Downtown Chwx   Low 1.6 High 6.8
6°C @ 0551 variable cloud slept 6½ hours   MILES/TIME
Sunrise 0755 Sunset 1615 Daylight 8:20

TUES.

COURSE/NOTES

Min 0.4 Max 6.8

°C @   Low 1.9 H 6.8
            slept 5½ hours   MILES/TIME
Sunrise 756 Sunset 1615 Daylight 8:19

WED.

COURSE/NOTES

Min   Max
Low 0.9 High 7.2
5°C @ 0706 Overcast slept 7 hours   MILES/TIME
Sunrise 0757 Sunset 1614 Daylight 8:17

THUR.

COURSE/NOTES

Min 2.8 Max 9.0

°C @   slept   MILES/TIME
Sunrise 075 Sunset 76 Daylight 8:

DATE Dec. 12 **FRI.**

COURSE/NOTES Walk 16.08.57, Run 3.46.17 before IT band
hurt on right leg, walk 3.30.10, Run 3.26.52 before IT
band hurt again; walk 5.06.71, Run 2.01.08 before IT
band hurt again; walk 3.41.27 home.

shadow 3 96.15

Low 1.1 High 6.8   4h
1°C @ 0605 Variable Clouds Slept 6¾ hours   37.40.42
Sunrise 0759 Sunset 1614   Daylight 8:15   MILES/TIME

DATE Dec. 13 **SAT.**

COURSE/NOTES Slept from 1215 to 0500 then
Slept from 0700 to 1630

Min 3.5 Max 7.6

°C @   Slept
Sunrise 0800   Sunset 1615   Daylight 8:15   MILES/TIME

DATE Dec. 14 **SUN.**

COURSE/NOTES Slept from 0130 to 0500 then off and
on to 0800

Min 4.6 Max 10.6
Low 1.4 High 7.0
3°C @ 0933 Overcast/windy Slept 5½ hours   MILES/TIME
Sunrise 0801   Sunset 1615   Daylight 8:14

REVIEW

GOALS/NOTES

WEIGHT   CUMULATIVE TOTAL   WEEKLY TOTAL

MON.

COURSE/NOTES Slept poorly. Shaun woke me up
2 or 3 times crying due to teething

Min 4.8 Max 8.8
Low 1.1 High 6.1
6°C @ 0658 Raining   Slept 6 3/4 hours   MILES/TIME
Sunrise 0801   Sunset 1615   Daylight 8:14

TUES.
DATE Dec. 16

COURSE/NOTES Feel like I might be getting sick
Feel like I need more sleep

Min 5.5 Max 11.0
Low 0.7 High 6.6
9°C @ 0700 Raining   Slept 8 1/2 hours   MILES/TIME
Sunrise 0802   Sunset 1615   Daylight 8:13

WED.
DATE Dec. 17

COURSE/NOTES Feel like I did not get enough sleep
woke up at 0530 could not sleep any longer.
Work is driving me nuts!

Min 4.8 Max 8.5
Low 0.5 High 6.3
8°C @ 0530 Overcast   Slept 6 hours   MILES/TIME
Sunrise 0803   Sunset 1615   Daylight 8:12

THUR.
DATE Dec. 18

COURSE/NOTES

windchill -2°C
2°C Downtown @ 0542   Min 2.4 Max 6.4
5°C @ 0545 some clouds   Low 0.6 High 6.2
                                 Slept 5 1/2 hours   MILES/TIME
Sunlight 0804   Sunset 1616   Daylight 8:12

DATE __Dec. 19__   **F**RI.

COURSE/NOTES _____
_____
_____
_____

40C @ 0715 Overcast   Min Low 0.6 Max High 6.2   Slept 7 1/2 hours   MILES/TIME
Sunrise 0804 Sunset 1616   Daylight 8:12

DATE __Dec. 20__   **S**AT.

COURSE/NOTES Slept 3 hours went to work at 0530
Slept 1 1/2 hours in the afternoon
_____
_____

                        Min 5.0 Max 8.6
                        Slept 3 hours   MILES/TIME
Sunrise   Sunset   Daylight

DATE __Dec. 21__ First Day of Winter   **S**UN.

COURSE/NOTES walked 22.42.33, Ran 3.10.93 IT band
started to hurt, also left foot outside below and
in front of my ankle hurt. walked 3.05.62, ran 3.18.15
IT band hurt again, walked 4.14.28. Total time 36.31.28
IT band on right leg hurts
                        Min 0.6 Max 5.8
-20C Downtown   Low   High   36.31.28
20C @ 0751 Clear Sunny Slept 7 1/4 hours   MILES/TIME
Sunset 0805 Sunset 1617 Daylight 8:12

                                                    REVIEW

GOALS/NOTES _____
_____
_____
_____
_____

WEIGHT [   ]   CUMULATIVE TOTAL [   ]   WEEKLY TOTAL [   ]

MON.

COURSE/NOTES Stretch and Strengthening

-30c windchill

Low 0.8 High 6.2 Min 1.8 Max 4.5
30c @ 0620 Raining lightly slept 5 3/4 hours   MILES/TIME
Sunrise 0806 Sunset 1617 Daylight 08:11

TUES.

COURSE/NOTES

                          Min 1.8 Max 5.5
windchill -4c   Low 0.7 High 6.1
30c @ 0658 Overcast   slept 7 1/4 hours   MILES/TIME
Sunrise 0806 Sunset 1618 Daylight 8:12

WED.

COURSE/NOTES

6 0c @ 1503 Sunny slept 7 1/2 hours   MILES/TIME
Sunrise 0807 Sunset 1619 Daylight 8:12

THUR.

COURSE/NOTES

30c @ 2114 Sunny slept 6 hours   MILES/TIME
Sunrise Sunset Daylight

DATE Dec.26   **F**RI.

COURSE/NOTES _____
_____
_____
_____
                    Min 0.3 Max 3.3
_____
                                         _____
                              MILES/TIME
Sunrise   Sunset   Daylight

DATE Dec.27   **S**AT.

COURSE/NOTES _____
_____
_____
_____
                         Min-1.2 Max 5.9
                   Low 0   High 50½ hours
1@0750 overcast   Slept 7 MILES/TIME
Sunrise 0807 Sunset 1621 Daylight 8:14

DATE Dec.28   **S**UN.

COURSE/NOTES Rode bike through UBC trail
→ 150m fog Deer fern from Huckelberry go to Hemlock
  and Huckelberry
- within first 150m of riding my right IT band hurt
  but it went away quickly and did not hurt later
                    Min 4.3 Max 10.5
                 Low 8.3 High 15.2   1:11:53
50C@0821 Raining Slept 8½hours   16.31
Sunrise 0808 Sunset 1622 Daylight 8:14

                                       REVIEW

GOALS/NOTES _____
_____
_____
_____
_____
_____

WEIGHT [   ]   CUMULATIVE [   ]   WEEKLY [   ]
                TOTAL   TOTAL
                                   ride 16.31m

MON.

DATE Dec. 29

COURSE/NOTES _____

Min 8.8 Max 11.2
Low -0.1 High 5.2

10°C @ 0758 Overcast Slept 7 3/4 | MILES/TIME |
Sunrise 0808 Sunset 1623 Daylight 8:15

TUES.

DATE Dec. 30

COURSE/NOTES _____

Min 4.7 Max 11.4
Low -0.4 High 5.3

9°C @ 0700 Overcast Slept 5 hours | MILES/TIME |
Sunrise 0808 Sunset 1623 Daylight 8:15

WED.

DATE Dec. 31

COURSE/NOTES _____

Min 1.8 Max 7.3
Low -0.7 High 5.4

3°C Downtown
4°C @ 0649 Fog Slept 7 hours | MILES/TIME |
Sunrise 0808 Sunset 1624 Daylight 8:16

THUR.

DATE Jan 1 9?

COURSE/NOTES _____

Min 1.9 Max 8.1
Low 0.6 High 5.2

windchill -5°C
4°C @ 1707 Rain Slept 7 hours | MILES/TIME |
Sunrise Sunset Daylight
sunrise 0804 Sunset 1625 Daylight 8:17

DATE _Jan. 2_   **F**RI.

COURSE/NOTES _____

_____

_____

_____

                Min   Max

10°C @ 0811 Variable Clouds Low -0.9 Sept 7½ low 4.7

Sunrise 0808 Sunset 1626 Daylight 8:18   MILES/TIME

DATE _Jan. 3_   **S**AT.

COURSE/NOTES _____

_____

_____

_____

_____ MILES/TIME

DATE _Jan. 4_   **S**UN.

COURSE/NOTES _____

_____

_____

_____

_____ MILES/TIME

REVIEW

GOALS/NOTES _____

_____

_____

_____

_____

WEIGHT   CUMULATIVE TOTAL   WEEKLY TOTAL

MON.

DATE _____

COURSE/NOTES _____
_____
_____
_____
_____
_____
_____   MILES/TIME [   ]

TUES.

DATE _____

COURSE/NOTES _____
_____
_____
_____
_____
_____
_____   MILES/TIME [   ]

WED.

DATE _____

COURSE/NOTES _____
_____
_____
_____
_____
_____
_____   MILES/TIME [   ]

THUR.

DATE _____

COURSE/NOTES _____
_____
_____
_____
_____
_____
_____   MILES/TIME [   ]

FRI.

DATE _____

COURSE/NOTES _____
_____
_____
_____
_____
_____
_____ MILES/TIME [   ]

SAT.

DATE _____

COURSE/NOTES _____
_____
_____
_____
_____
_____
_____ MILES/TIME [   ]

SUN.

DATE _____

COURSE/NOTES _____
_____
_____
_____
_____
_____
_____ MILES/TIME [   ]

REVIEW

GOALS/NOTES _____
_____
_____
_____
_____
_____

WEIGHT [   ]   CUMULATIVE TOTAL [   ]   WEEKLY TOTAL [   ]

MON.

DATE _____

COURSE/NOTES _____
_____
_____
_____
_____
_____
_____ MILES/TIME

TUES.

DATE _____

COURSE/NOTES _____
_____
_____
_____
_____
_____
_____ MILES/TIME

WED.

DATE _____

COURSE/NOTES _____
_____
_____
_____
_____
_____
_____ MILES/TIME

THUR.

DATE _____

COURSE/NOTES _____
_____
_____
_____
_____
_____
_____ MILES/TIME

FRI.

DATE _____

COURSE/NOTES _____
_____
_____
_____
_____
_____ MILES/TIME [   ]

SAT.

DATE _____

COURSE/NOTES _____
_____
_____
_____
_____
_____ MILES/TIME [   ]

SUN.

DATE _____

COURSE/NOTES _____
_____
_____
_____
_____
_____ MILES/TIME [   ]

REVIEW

GOALS/NOTES _____
_____
_____
_____
_____

WEIGHT [   ]   CUMULATIVE TOTAL [   ]   WEEKLY TOTAL [   ]

MON.

DATE _____

COURSE/NOTES _____
_____
_____
_____
_____
_____
_____ MILES/TIME

TUES.

DATE _____

COURSE/NOTES _____
_____
_____
_____
_____
_____
_____ MILES/TIME

WED.

DATE _____

COURSE/NOTES _____
_____
_____
_____
_____
_____
_____ MILES/TIME

THUR.

DATE _____

COURSE/NOTES _____
_____
_____
_____
_____
_____
_____ MILES/TIME

FRI.

DATE _____

COURSE/NOTES _____
_____
_____
_____
_____
_____
_____ MILES/TIME [   ]

SAT.

DATE _____

COURSE/NOTES _____
_____
_____
_____
_____
_____
_____ MILES/TIME [   ]

SUN.

DATE _____

COURSE/NOTES _____
_____
_____
_____
_____
_____
_____ MILES/TIME [   ]

REVIEW

GOALS/NOTES _____
_____
_____
_____
_____
_____

WEIGHT [   ]   CUMULATIVE TOTAL [   ]   WEEKLY TOTAL [   ]

Michelle Dimuro in the 1992 Olympic Trials 800 meter heat.

"He who has health has hope, and he who has hope has everything."

-*Arabian proverb*